If you want your students to experience the authenticity (it's real!), the productivity (they learn more and better!), and the sheer joy (they love it!) of learning to read *and* write together, seamlessly, and synergistically—and do it all in a studio setting (where they are the artists!)—then Ellin Keene's *The Literacy Studio* is the book for you. As a bonus, you'll experience the same authenticity, productivity, and joy as a teacher (and learner!) in the studio.

—P. David Pearson

Ellin Oliver Keene

The Literacy Studio

Redesigning the Workshop for Readers _and_ Writers

HEINEMANN
Portsmouth, NH

Heinemann
145 Maplewood Avenue, Suite 300
Portsmouth, NH 03801
www.heinemann.com

The author and publisher wish to thank those who have generously given permission to reprint borrowed material:

p. 19 Excerpt from "Time Spent Reading and Reading Growth" by Barbara M. Taylor, Barbara J. Frye, and Geoffrey M. Maruyama from *American Educational Research Journal*, Summer 1990, Vol. 27, No. 2. Copyright © 1990. Reprinted by permission of the Copyright Clearance Center on behalf of SAGE Publications, Inc.

Acknowledgments for borrowed material continue on p. vi.

Library of Congress Cataloging-in-Publication Data
Names: Keene, Ellin Oliver, author.
Title: The literacy studio : redesigning the workshop for readers and
   writers / Ellin Oliver Keene.
Description: Portsmouth, NH : Heinemann, [2022] | Includes bibliographical
   references.
Identifiers: LCCN 2022022683 | ISBN 9780325120058
Subjects: LCSH: Language arts (Elementary) | Literacy programs. | Active
   learning. | Student-centered learning.
Classification: LCC LB1576 .K384 2022 | DDC 372.6—dc23/eng/20220617
LC record available at https://lccn.loc.gov/2022022683

Editor: Tom Newkirk
Production: Victoria Merecki
Cover and interior designs: Monica Ann Cohen
Typesetting: Gina Poirier, Gina Poirier Design
Manufacturing: Val Cooper

Printed in the United States of America on acid-free paper.
1 2 3 4 5 VP 26 25 24 23 22 PO 34909

To Milagro,
with love

Credits, *continued from page iv*

p. 22 Excerpt from "Engagement with Young Adult Literature: Outcomes and Processes" by Gay Ivey and Peter H. Johnston from *Reading Research Quarterly* Vol. 48, No. 3. Copyright © 2013. Reprinted by permission of the Copyright Clearance Center on behalf of John Wiley & Sons, Inc.

Figure 2.1 Excerpt from *Talk About Understanding: Rethinking Classroom Talk to Enhance Comprehension* by Ellin Oliver Keene. Copyright © 2012 by Ellin Oliver Keene. Published by Heinemann, Portsmouth, NH. Reprinted by permission of the publisher. All rights reserved.

pp. 119, 146–147 Excerpts from the Common Core State Standards. © Copyright 2010. National Governors Association Center for Best Practices and Council of Chief State School Officers. All rights reserved.

p. 181 Republished with permission of the Association for Supervision & Curriculum Development, from *Essential Questions: Opening Doors to Student Understanding* by Jay McTighe and Grant P. Wiggins, © 2013. Permission conveyed through Copyright Clearance Center, Inc.

Image Credits

Cover: Michael Landry (photos); © Rudchenko Liliia/Shutterstock/HIP (watercolors)

Interior: Michael Landry (pages xv, 9, 23, 67, 86, 94, 117, 145, 152, 175, 177, 189); © Barry Winiker/Getty Images (page 2); Lisa Fowler (pages 13, 19, 55, 59, 185)

Contents

Acknowledgments   x

Prelude   xiv

◆ Welcome to the Literacy Studio, an update to reader's and writer's workshops.

Chapter 1 Why Literacy Studio?   1

◆ Why should we change our current practices in reader's and writer's workshops?

◆ What does the research say?

◆ **Integrating reading and writing:** How do we plan for Literacy Studio by integrating concepts from reading *and* writing?

◆ **Choice:** Providing more choice to foster engagement

◆ **Time:** How can we create more time for students to engage in independent reading and writing?

Chapter 2 Time for a Reboot   11

◆ Sound familiar? Issues facing teachers and learners in reader's and writer's workshop classrooms

◆ How is Literacy Studio different from other types of classroom literacy/workshop models?

◆ The time conundrum

◆ The history of reader's and writer's workshop: What worked for a while and why

◆ Is there an alternative when we have constraining demands such as time and too much content to teach?

Chapter 3 It's All About the Planning!   31

◆ The planning wheel: A tool to integrate reading and writing

◆ How do we think about planning for Literacy Studio?

◆ The components of Literacy Studio, briefly explained

◆ What does Literacy Studio look like, day to day, month to month, across a school year?

Chapter 4 All Together Now: Exploring the Craft of the Reader and Writer in Crafting Sessions   57

◆ Minilessons become Crafting Sessions

◆ The time dilemma

◆ What, exactly, is a Crafting Session?

◆ An in-depth look at a Crafting Session

Chapter 5 From Crafting to Composing: How It All Comes Together   83

◆ Brushes: Your instructional moves

◆ Paint colors: Important learning targets for readers and writers

◆ Canvases: Materials to make your Literacy Studio shine

Chapter 6 The Heart of Literacy Studio: Independent Composing   111

◆ Composing: Independent and small-group work

◆ The potency of our language

◆ Planning for Composing

◆ A primary Composing Session

◆ An intermediate Composing Session

Chapter 7 Composing: How It All Comes Together 142

- ◆ Launching Literacy Studio for the first time
- ◆ Conferring in Literacy Studio
- ◆ Invitational groups in Literacy Studio

Chapter 8 Reflection: The Home for Important Questions and Life Lessons 174

- ◆ Using global questions in Literacy Studio
- ◆ Children as teachers: A new take on reflection
- ◆ The joy of sharing

Postlude 197

Appendix 1: Planning Wheel 202
Appendix 2: Record-Keeping Forms 203

References 211

Additional Resources Available Online:

- ◆ Essential Conditions for Literacy Studio
- ◆ Sample Lessons
- ◆ Thinking Strategies and Writer's Tools

To download the Appendices and additional online resources, please visit **http://hein.pub/LitStudio** and click on **Companion Resources**.

ACKNOWLEDGMENTS

So many splendid educators have had a hand in the development of the ideas in this book. Even if I somehow recaptured my twenty-one-year-old memory, I'm afraid I would never remember all, but I am beyond grateful to teachers around the country who have implemented Literacy Studio and work every year to refine it. It's also true that the birth of these ideas in my long-ago classrooms involved my amazing students; I owe them so much credit.

I would like to thank my colleagues at Tillman Elementary in Palmetto, Florida. Jill Bradley, instructional coach, and principal Marla Massi-Blackmore asked vital and sometimes confounding questions that pushed my thinking. You'll visit classrooms at Tillman throughout this book. Prepare to be amazed!

My deepest thanks as well to my beloved colleagues in Fort Osage, Missouri: Blue Hills, Buckner, Cler-Mont, Elm Grove, and Indian Trails Elementary Schools, and Fire Prairie Upper Elementary. The educators there are inspiring; you'll hear their voices throughout this book and will find yourself wishing to be in their classrooms. Believe me, it is a gift I don't take for granted. I am particularly grateful to instructional coaches Tyler Dierking, Ryann Carlson, Krissy Smith, Andrea Ryan, Kristi Odell, and Erica Wood and assistant superintendent Emily Cross for their spirit of adventure in making Literacy Studio come to life. Prior to her retirement Maria Fleming, assistant superintendent, was a tremendous support and I miss her.

During the writing of this book, I've developed wonderful colleagueship with teachers, coaches, and principals around the Grand Rapids, Michigan, area. Diane Titche, who developed an extraordinary initiative around my last book, *Engaging Children*, has been my steadfast thought partner and dear friend. I'd also like to thank Mike Birely, principal extraordinaire at

Appleview Elementary in Sparta, Michigan, and his colleagues Katherine Ley, Kelley Van Vliet, and Sherry Kilpatrick, who have been a joy to observe as they implement Literacy Studio. Bridget Reith, Christy Gast, and principal Caroline Cannon at Breton Downs Elementary in East Grand Rapids have distinguished themselves as leaders in the initiative. I look forward to so much more learning alongside each of them and their wonderful colleagues.

There are so many other educators I want to thank, but above all, I will never find adequate words to express my thanks to colleagues and dear friends at Milagro Charter School in downtown Los Angeles. The photographs you see on the cover and many throughout this book come from Milagro where we have worked side by side to create beautiful Literacy Studios and to address every aspect of literacy learning for the extraordinary Milagro children. Relish, as I do, the photos from these amazing classrooms and think about the educators behind those engaged faces. Sascha Robinett's and Martha Moran's leadership from the principal's office is nothing short of groundbreaking. I have rarely seen such inspirational, thoughtful, and *knowledgeable* leadership in my many decades in education. These leaders have made it possible for teachers Julissa Alarcon, Gabriela Calderon, Nadia Cardenas, Daniela Encarnacion, Aurora Escarsega, Renae Hernandez, Carol Lopez, Lisa Soto Michelob, Janessa Perez, Fabviola Rosales, Anna Suarez, and Hortensia Toledo to soar in their classrooms and they do. I am proud to thank Karla Contreras, second-grade teacher, and Modesta Urbina, third-grade teacher, who have joined me in providing professional learning for teachers throughout the country—their thinking enriches mine in every conversation. I proudly invite any colleague in the field to visit Milagro, any classroom, any time. If I didn't know how much hard work has gone into the learning there, I would be tempted to think it was magic.

The bulk of this book was written during the COVID-19 quarantine when we all faced a world so unfamiliar, confusing, and tragic. My deepest thanks to my stalwart colleagues who are dear friends: Carl Anderson, Katherine Bomer, Kathy Collins, Dan Feigelson, Towanda Harris, Aeriale Johnson, Jessica Martin, Vicki Vinton, and Janet Zarchan. I learned more from these colleagues in that relatively short time than I can begin to describe. Ironically, it was our stasis that made it possible to deeply engage with one another, ask critical questions about literacy learning, race, equity, and justice. The learning curve was and remains steep, and I would give anything if many of our conversations hadn't been prompted by the horrendous violence that took the lives of so many people of color including George Floyd, Ahmaud Arbery, Breonna Taylor, and far too many since. Through heartbreak and tough conversation, we thought together about what we could contribute to children, teachers, and our communities. It's a work in progress and I'm enormously grateful to these colleagues for their ideas, and their candor and patience.

Georgia Heard and Matt Glover have been air and water for me through the confounding last few years. We've worked closely together in a variety of contexts and have generated new knowledge together. They challenge my thinking and offer warm friendship, a rare combination indeed. Thanks to both for reading this book ahead of publication.

Many years ago, at the founding of the Public Education & Business Coalition, I was privileged to work alongside Anne Goudvis, Stephanie Harvey, Debbie Miller, and Cris Tovani. For years we passed each other in airports and wished that we had time to talk. The isolation of the pandemic provided the time and we met regularly to study equity and justice, plan for professional learning, and mostly laugh out loud, talk at the same time, and develop gratitude for the decades of learning and friendship we've had. Debbie kindly agreed to read this book ahead of publication. Her insights are treasures.

I would like to offer my deepest thanks to Tom Newkirk, who worked alongside me as my editor. Tom's genius is well known to the readers of this book. Imagine for a moment how intimidating it is to have one's early drafts read by such a great mind and stirring writer. I had to just get over it, and we had one heck of a roller-coaster ride with this book. It was hard! Tom pushed me to do one simple thing: Make the book understandable to its readers. Not so simple and I would be utterly adrift without him. I dedicated one book to him, I dare not do so again lest he become unbearable for his wonderful wife, Beth, to live with. Suffice to say, every single one of my books should be dedicated to Tom Newkirk.

I would also like to thank my Heinemann team, particularly Kim Cahill, Victoria Merecki, and Monica Cohen. I believe the children and teachers whose stories I tell here deserve an aesthetically beautiful, well-edited book and that's what they're getting.

My sweet little family continues to sustain and encourage me as I write and travel to be in schools. My husband David has supported me and made me laugh and think for nearly four decades. My nephew Edward, whom I consider a son, and his wife Alyson who will very shortly (after this book is out) bring my first grandchild to the world. I love them dearly and will spoil this kid rotten! My daughter, Elizabeth Keene, who works in publishing has been invaluable writing support along with being just the best daughter a mom could ever have. She is brave, brave, brave—also brilliant and loving and the greatest gift of my life.

Welcome to the Literacy Studio!

This book is about authenticity. It is about how we can transform students' literacy learning into a process that aligns more closely with what readers and writers do outside an academic setting. My own reading and writing life, my identity in the realm of literacy and yours, drive what we teach and how we teach when we're working with young readers and writers. I know that if we build upon a lifetime of experiences as readers and writers, our teaching and their learning will be more authentic. When we pause to consider our lives as literate people, though, it isn't always a fairy tale.

When I bring my life as a reader into the classroom, I know that my experiences, and I'm guessing yours as well, won't always fit the standard narrative of a reader who cozies up with a book on a snowy afternoon, fire crackling in the background with no distractions. Some of my experiences are anchored in the ideal; many are not. I worry that we represent ourselves as unflawed literacy models when the truth is that reading is challenging, though ultimately gratifying beyond measure for most of us. I catch time to read when I can. I may be in the middle of a great novel, but when my eyelids feel heavy, I prioritize sleep—I'm going to be in classrooms at zero-dark-thirty the next day!

My goal is for our students to prioritize reading the way we do—as a choice made with the full knowledge that they must ignore or postpone the distractions and items on the to-do list to read. I want kids to gradually build a commitment to reading over their years in school. To work toward that goal, ragged edges and all, we're going to have to be honest with children. Let's think for a moment about a child who doesn't identify as a proficient reader and writer and who frequently hears us talk in exultant terms about reading. Are they feeling disconnected, less than? I want that child to know that, even for those of us who love books and language, there is struggle in the process and struggle is something worth embracing. The payoff is more than worth the bumpy process it takes to engage as readers.

Understanding a writer's life is critical as well, and I make sure that I share my writing life with kids, good, bad, and ugly, whenever I can. I shared this prelude, as I was drafting it, with several groups of students in grades 3–5 in the autumn of 2021. We were all trying to find our way back to some facsimile of the school we had known before the pandemic, and it was a struggle. It struck me that this is a time to be very honest with kids about what writers do.

I've found that most kids see writing as a rough draft, edit (punctuation, spelling, grammar), second draft, turn-it-in kind of process. I love to be the

one who disavows that conception of writing. I tell them, perhaps too bluntly, "You were misinformed. Here's another way to look at the writing process." I tell them that I must have dozens of conversations with teachers, with my editor, Tom Newkirk, with other trusted colleagues, and I have to write and rewrite and delete, delete, delete. I surprise them every time when I tell them that I cut close to half of what I write. I put the rejected words into a file euphemistically called "Later," but it's rare that something in Later makes it to the final product. Still, I feel better knowing those words are still there. I tell kids that I revise as I write rather than going back and doing another draft. My guess is that most writers do the same.

This fall, I wondered aloud if other authors write the introduction or, my preferred term, *prelude*, last. I tell kids, and you'll soon learn, that this book was born in the Rose Reading Room in the main branch of the New York Public Library, but I certainly didn't start with the prelude. Why do we expect kids to write meaningfully, draft 1, draft 2, publish? Writing remains an act of discovery for me, and I hope we encourage students to discover as they write. I really don't know; I *can't* know what a book is going to be until I'm well into it. When it's time to write the prelude the book is largely written, I'm tired and very self-critical. No one will ever read this drivel! My beloved father died in August 2021; one of the things I miss the most is his little adages and witticisms. When I was in the self-doubting stage at the end of writing a book, he always said, "Honey, don't worry. I'll buy ten copies and that will put your sales in double digits!" Thanks, Dad.

As a writer, I can't know if this book will be meaningful, will lead to any welcome changes in your classroom, will sell! But I do know that I have a down-to-my-core belief in teachers; when you find ideas that make sense for your kids, you'll move heaven and earth to bring them to life in your classroom.

In the true-confessions category, I must also acknowledge that I don't often read introductions to books. If I do read one, it's because I'm looking back to try to understand the book's structure. It's important for kids to know that.

I mention my struggles and propensities with my reading and writing to indicate that this book is about creating a lively, honest, authentic approach to teaching literacy that makes sense to kids. To do that, we must be honest about our identities, struggles, and joys as readers and writers, no matter how we approach literacy teaching and learning.

So, if you are the one person who is actually reading this, thank you. You alone will know that the prelude was written last and that I've learned to put most of the content in the chapters! So, permit me to say a word or two about the structure of *The Literacy Studio*. I can only hope that it will make as much sense to you as it does for me now that I'm done putting all the puzzle pieces in place.

> To walk into a classroom and have students eager to share what they are writing, reading, or discovering has been the needed joy in a myriad of challenges this year. Witnessing the students' confidence build because they can feel their own growth as readers and writers is something beyond test scores, it is the foundation of lifelong learning and the reason why we teach.
>
> —Sascha Robinett, Principal, Milagro Elementary School, Los Angeles, CA

In Chapter 1 of *The Literacy Studio*, I'll argue that we are ready, as teachers, to refine and build upon the traditional reader's and writer's workshop to create an integrated Literacy Studio that makes more sense to kids, is supported by the research, and saves us a whole lot of time.

In Chapter 2, I'll begin by examining what has worked well and must be preserved in the classic reader's and writer's workshop before suggesting alternatives.

In Chapter 3, we'll take on the all-important question of planning for the Literacy Studio. I'll suggest an almost impossibly simple, yet incredibly flexible, planning tool I learned from my colleague and friend Debbie Miller, literacy consultant and first-grade teacher extraordinaire. I'll share some plans that I've used in classrooms. I'll suggest a yearlong trajectory for integrating reading and writing as you consider the units you teach each year.

In Chapter 4, we'll dig into the first of four components of the Literacy Studio: whole-class instruction, which we'll call a Crafting Session. I'll guide you through the very specific course of one Crafting Session to expose the ins and outs of integrating reading and writing.

Chapter 5 will provide dozens of practical tools for implementing the Literacy Studio components (like Crafting) I've described in the even-numbered chapters. In Chapter 5, we'll look at the content we teach (the what), the instructional strategies we use (the how), and the materials we use to integrate reading and writing. There you'll see at least one reading and writing standard for each grade, K–5, with a suggestion about how to integrate them and a selection of texts to use.

In Chapter 6, we'll delve into the heart of the Literacy Studio, the Composing Session (independent work time). You'll join me for a primary lesson in which a teacher and I integrate reading and writing, and you'll join me for some conferences in which I strive to help individual students make those reading-writing connections. We'll also take a look at Composing time in a fourth-grade classroom.

Chapter 7 will provide implementation-ready tools to flesh out Composing Sessions including details on conferring in the Literacy Studio, and the third component of the Literacy Studio: Invitational Groups (small, needs-based groups). I'll invite you to join an Invitational Group from a third-grade classroom.

In Chapter 8, we'll explore the Reflecting Session, the fourth component of the Literacy Studio. We'll investigate the ways that global questions, students as teachers, and focused sharing can ground the students' work in a more equitable social world and in the ever-changing natural world where you'll start to think about how to integrate social studies, inquiry, and science into your Literacy Studio.

Finally, in the postlude, I'll invite you to make the Literacy Studio your own. My greatest wish is that, after reading this book, you'll find my ideas valuable enough to *change* them. Each of us needs to have that kitchen-table moment when we decide to make the changes in our classrooms that will lead to greater student involvement and engagement. You already know about reader's and writer's workshops—you've heard about them in your teacher education programs; perhaps you've implemented a workshop approach to literacy. Maybe you're just trying to fine-tune an already strong version of workshop teaching in your classroom. All are welcome in the Literacy Studio!

CHAPTER ONE

Why Literacy Studio?

This book was born in the Rose Main Reading Room of the New York Public Library. The library, at 42nd Street and 5th Avenue, is home to the huge concrete lions, Patience and Fortitude, that rest on either side of the steps leading into the spectacular building. The Reading Room is 297 feet long, roughly the length of one city block, and its interior is one of the most iconic public spaces in the city where, if I'm honest, I am happiest. I have never chosen the birthplace of a book intentionally, but for this one I wanted to capture my first ideas alone in the presence of others, a phrase that has always spoken to me. It suggests that meaningful work in the mind happens best, side by side with those who are deeply engrossed in their books, their newspapers, their writing. It suggests a community, nearby but slightly apart. It suggests a studio of sorts, a hive of cognitive activity, discovery, expression, and some healthy staring into space.

Alone in the presence of others is where I wanted to collect my earliest ideas for this book—among other thinkers, people from every conceivable walk of life who had come to that spot for the silence and the white noise of clicking keys and sighs, overheard conversation, coughing, and the rustle of newsprint. I wanted to be among those who have peopled this hallowed space every day for years and years, people who have grown old in the same, almost soft wood swivel chairs; I wanted to be among those to whom the habit of thinking and rethinking is air and water.

The Reading Room suggests a tone I want to strike in classrooms—a thriving birthplace for ideas from text, great conversation (which no longer must be whispered, at least on one side of the Reading Room), and the emergence of a writer's words on a page. In the Reading Room, all those things happen simultaneously. A reader swerves into writing for a few minutes and then returns to reading. The writer pours through pages in books, seeking and finding inspiration, and, with no perceptible change in purpose, turns back to generating their own text, and returns to reading.

As my fingers began to move across the keyboard that day, I wrote, "In literacy teaching and learning, we want to foster authenticity and a sense of possibility—students choose their topics and books; we work alongside each other in service of the children's goals as readers and writers. There is a sense of freedom to experiment with language, but it comes with serious engagement, a commitment to trying what they've learned from the teacher and other readers and writers, and a sense of responsibility for each other. I imagine (and have seen!) classrooms where there is a palpable sense of possibility; we can't wait to hear what kids have to say about books and we hold our breath as they share their writing. There is just no doubt that they are going to dazzle us. We know they will, and they don't disappoint. We teach the essential concepts in literacy; we align those concepts to their needs. We trust kids."

These early jottings transported me back to my own classroom, to a year when I was teaching fifth grade. I harbored some of the same hopes as I've just shared, but at that moment I was beyond frustrated and beginning to believe that I was incompetent. Perhaps I should get a job as a ski instructor (in my dreams!). My literacy block wasn't working. I was trying to ensure that my students had enough time to read and write each day; I knew I had to address my district's curriculum goals; I was woefully short on time to confer with students; I didn't feel like I had a solid understanding of their progress; they almost never had time to share; moving toward a solution in one area felt like I had opened a can of worms in the others. When it was time for spring break, I was bone-tired, and I was just damn well going to ski every day of the break,

But that was the year of way too little snow in Colorado. If that had been the year of just enough snow, or an abundance of snow, the Literacy Studio might never have been born.

I sat at home that spring break and became more downtrodden. I was a lousy teacher *and* there was no snow? C'mon, unfair universe, give a girl a break! It was an exercise in self-pity about which I am not proud, but it led to the moment when I sat down at my kitchen table and decided to sketch out some new schedules, to start fresh. I am a bit aghast at my audacity to just rethink everything about my literacy instruction in a week, but that's exactly what I did. Ah, youth. I reasoned that if I tried an entirely new approach in the last quarter of that year, I would learn what needed to be amended for the fall of the next school year. I wasn't wrong.

I called our reboot Literacy Studio. It was designed mainly to buy me some more time to confer, but I came to realize that the new structure made far more sense to kids and reinvigorated the whole literacy block in a way I couldn't have imagined. I clearly remember the day I greeted my kids after spring break and announced with great fanfare that they were now part of a Literacy Studio. I made it sound like something real and important, not something I made up at my kitchen table!

What was a Literacy Studio? I told them it meant that we would be working as readers and writers throughout the time set aside for literacy. It meant that, whenever possible, I would teach reading and writing together in one lesson. It meant that they could—gasp—*choose* when to read and when to write if they could ensure that they gave equal time to both. They *loved* that part. It meant that they would have more time to talk with each other about books and their writing and that they would take more responsibility for choosing their books and writing topics. They *loved* that part too.

We fumbled through that quarter together and met frequently to discuss how it was going. What if they wanted to read for three days in a row and then write for three days in a row? What if they wanted to read the same book with a friend? What if they wanted to coauthor a piece with a friend? How could they make sharing time less, well, boring? We felt like problem-solvers, putting our heads together to make this important time of the day more meaningful. I felt the sense of possibility seep back into our work. I felt more confident. I was a little worried that I'd just gone rogue in my school, but none of my team members were on board, so I just went for it. I have an ongoing problem with authority—ask any family member—so I loved that part. I was going my own way to make the workshop work for us.

Take a moment to visualize the scene that is the norm in many American reader's and writer's workshops today. How do children currently experience much of their work as readers and writers? The workshop often begins with the students gathering to hear a wonderful read-aloud; the teacher shares their thinking and perhaps invites the students to talk about what they've discovered about themselves as readers, the goals they're working toward.

Then everyone transitions into independent reading and starts reading; some may lose focus for a time, some regain it and resume reading, and some may or may not lose focus again; then it's time to put their books away. Finally, they all gather again to listen to some students share, take a quick stretch break, and . . . repeat the whole process with a writing lesson. Two lessons. Four transitions. A limited time to dig into their independent reading or writing. Lather, rinse, repeat!

At Indian Trails, we got started with Literacy Studio by first working on our classroom environment. Teachers started letting students work on their reading and writing around the room and joined them in their workspaces for conferring. We learned to create lessons that teach the reader and the writer, which were based on a lot more modeling and thinking aloud. We noticed that students get started more quickly and stamina has increased.

—Kristi Odell, Instructional Coach, Indian Trails Elementary, Fort Osage, MO

Many teachers have grown frustrated with some elements of their literacy workshop and just wish they could design the workshop in a way that more fully meets *their students' needs*. I know—obviously, I felt the same way in my own classroom. The two most frustrating issues among my colleagues are that students don't have enough time for independent reading and writing and that they find it difficult to confer as often as they would like. They long for a workshop structure that is more flexible—one they can adjust week by week, month by month depending on their students' goals, progress, temperaments, and needs.

There are other vexing questions, particularly about the separate silos in which we currently work in reader's and writer's workshops:

- What led us to teach reading and writing separately? Given the inextricable ties between oral and written language, reading and writing, listening and speaking, why would we provide instruction on one at a time?

- Does it make sense to students to focus on reading and writing separately?

- Aren't there ways that reading and writing standards and curriculum align?

- When we long to provide more time for students to read and write independently, more time to confer with individuals, why would we teach two lessons a day, endure four transitions, and try to get some sharing time squeezed in? Doesn't that structure consume too much of the time we hope our students will spend actually reading and writing?

- What impact do separate reading and writing times have on student engagement?

There are so many more. Let's just look at that first question: What led us to teach reading and writing separately?

Do you remember your own elementary experience? Most of us experienced reading and writing as separate subjects. In fact, in my intermediate-grade years, I had different teachers for reading and writing, as many elementary students do today. Even in the most ideal circumstances where teachers plan together and communicate well, what conclusions do students draw as they pack up their writing materials and tromp down the hall to a different reading teacher? I worry that they, like I did at their age, see reading and writing as two entirely different disciplines.

I know I didn't make connections from the books I read to my own writing. I was a kid who loved to write, so I wrote stories at home because most of my "writing" classes had more to do with conventions, punctuation, and grammar than they did with encouraging us to create. There were so many missed opportunities, ways my teachers might have connected reading and writing. I don't want today's students to miss that integration.

These questions have troubled me for some time. In fact, I have a difficult time understanding why we persist in separating reading and writing. Do we teach reading and writing separately because published programs separate them? Maybe it's because we assess reading and writing separately? Are we "preparing them for middle school" by having them walk down the hall in a passing period? Is it related to our tendency to follow one approach in reading and another in writing? The fact is that we *have* separated reading and writing instruction to a greater or lesser degree, and it is past time to rethink it. We can do better for students, and we can regain control over the tyranny of the clock at the same time.

Perhaps you're wondering if research supports the integration of reading and writing. Guess what? We've had research for decades (e.g., Tierney and Pearson 1983; Knapp 1995; Morrow et al. 1999; Pressley et al. 1997; Wharton-McDonald, Pressley, and Hampston 1998) that suggests that teachers capitalize on the symbiotic relationship between reading and writing.

Graham (2017), for example, found that the more time elementary students spent writing and the more writing instruction they received, the more robust their gains in comprehension of texts. He argued, as have many others, that when students are reading, they can learn to think about the author (become metacognitive) and can focus on ways in which the author is manipulating (I'm going to use the word *manipulating* throughout this book as a positive thing that writers do!) their thinking. Those skills can, in turn, be used when it is the student's turn to compose. In his podcast, Graham goes on to say that "current understanding in the field of literacy dictates that reading and writing mutually reinforce one another and rely on some of the same cognitive processes." He cites Fitzgerald and Shanahan (2000); Shanahan (2006); and Tierney and Shanahan (1991). This insight suggests that instruction may be more effective when teachers integrate reading and writing experiences in the classroom. Tierney and Shanahan (253) suggest that "exemplary teachers who produce high-achieving readers and writers tend to integrate the two domains regularly and thoroughly in the classroom."

Many of us have long seen the wisdom in connecting reading and writing, but we don't usually *plan* to integrate instruction. If something related to writing occurs to us while teaching a reading lesson, we might mention it. If we're reading and writing in the same genre, we might study some mentor texts to help students improve their writing, but we often aren't intentional about the integration. It's difficult to remember to make the connection—if we aren't planning integrated lessons, do we imagine that students will automatically and seamlessly connect what they learn in separate writing and reading lessons? Do we imagine that they will pause to think, "Hmm, I'm learning that writers introduce characters through exposition, action, and dialogue. I think I'll need to consider how the author of the book I'm reading does the same"? Hmm, maybe not!

We want so much for our students. We want them to connect reading and writing; we want them to have more choice; we want them to have much more time to read and write. I don't know a teacher who doesn't value integration, choice, and time! And I know plenty who have taken the plunge; they have rearranged their literacy block structures to meet those three important goals, which are, not coincidentally, the three goals of this book!

1. We want students to see *the connections* between the books they read and their work as writers. We want these connections to be more than a happy accident. We want students to move seamlessly between reading and writing gleaning insight from both, even at the earliest grade levels.

2. We want students to have more *choice* in the texts they read and the topics about which they write, because choice often leads to deeper and more sustained engagement.

3. Perhaps most importantly, we want students to have more *time* to read and write each day—that's how they get better!

If those are the goals to which we aspire in our literacy workshops, we need to make the connections between reading and writing explicit. We need to teach students *how* to choose the texts they read and the topics about which they write. When they can choose texts and topics, we can invite them to choose *when* they read and *when* they write. And because we know (Allington 2011) that reading and writing independently is the single most important variable in student growth, we simply must carve out more time in the day for them to *practice* as readers and writers.

But how? In *The Literacy Studio*, I will reconsider our most basic assumptions about the "traditional" reader's and writer's workshop approach and structure. I will pose even more vexing questions that have caused me to rethink many of my assumptions about reader's workshop and writer's workshop. I will challenge some of the dogma that we often find in packaged programs that provide scripts and walk us through reader's and writer's workshop structures and, spoiler alert, I will argue that we can do much better for children.

In this book, I'll propose an alternative workshop structure, one you can adjust, amend, tinker with. Imagine a literacy block that is flexible enough to allow you to be directly responsive to your kids' needs. We're going to get down to the nitty-gritty detail about planning, scheduling, conferring, differentiating, record keeping, and reflecting so that your students can build their knowledge of reading by writing and vice versa. We'll talk about how to maximize students' choice in how they spend their time—yes, even little kids—and engagement as independent readers and writers.

The Literacy Studio takes teachers and children beyond the workshop structures that we've used for many years by maximizing time for active learning, and because reading and writing instruction is *integrated*, the daily literacy block often comprises just one lesson focusing on reading *and* writing. The Literacy Studio can cut instructional time in half and double its effectiveness. In integrated lessons built on, but not limited to, state standards, students learn to read with an eye to the author, thinking about what the author was up to and how they can use the same tools and strategies in their own work,

Modesta Urbina and Third-Grade Students

and they write with a specific reading audience sitting on their shoulder. They ask: "What do my readers need to think about to understand the message that is so important I've chosen to write about it?"

To make these changes is a bit of a daunting prospect, which is why I've worked side by side with teachers for years to figure this out in a wide variety of schools. And as you read, it's important to know that the vast majority of schools in which I work most serve low-income populations. I won't say that the Literacy Studio as I describe it in this book is perfected, but together we've sorted so many of the knottiest (and naughtiest) problems, and this book is all about sharing those solutions. We have learned that we can breathe new life and possibility into the reader's and writer's workshop to engage students and meet them where they are, including children who are new to English and students who have learning differences. We've developed ways to integrate reading and writing in both instruction and student application, and in so doing, reclaim time for them to work as readers and writers.

Finding time for independent work was the main reason I sat down to refresh our literacy time that snowless week in March years ago. I wanted to know that there was enough time to dig into relevant, differentiated instruction; deep levels of student engagement; and connections between reading and writing that will last a lifetime. I want the same for you and your students.

In a Literacy Studio students work as artists do, in a studio environment focused on work about which they feel passionate, in which they have a hand in setting their own direction, and (most of the time) choice about when and how to read, write, and show their thinking. Like an artist's studio, it is a bit messy at the beginning, but the new structures open much more time for you and your students. Like artists, students in a Literacy Studio are driven by the habit of revision; in a Literacy Studio, revision is revered. We are lucky to reread, rethink our writing; revising our thinking is a gift!

I'm glad I didn't get to ski that spring break week. I'm glad I was naive enough to think I could change the whole literacy block in one short week. I'm grateful to the students and colleagues who, that year and every year since, have helped me refine the Literacy Studio. Learning reading and writing together makes sense to kids.

CHAPTER TWO

Time for a Reboot

Sound Familiar? Issues Facing Teachers and Students in Reader's and Writer's Workshop Classrooms

It's a bright autumn morning in your elementary classroom, early in the year, so much ahead—nothing quite like those early days of promise. Literacy is first up for the day. You present a short minilesson (keep it snappy!) in reading and hustle the children off to read independently. You worry that it has taken too long this fall to get all your students into the "right" books, but they're reading for longer periods of time each day and finally you are ready to dig into real conferences. You rush to confer with as many students as possible. Just two today. There is simply never enough time. You have the students quickly share with a partner.

You are determined not to neglect writer's workshop this year. Last year it seemed that writing always took a back seat to reading, and the writing you did was almost always set up as an assignment, a response to text with very little emphasis on the students' original writing. So, you roll out a carefully planned writing minilesson using a wonderful mentor text, but it is, like most, unrelated to the reading lesson. This nags at you and you consider trying to make a connection to your earlier reading lesson, but you feel the press of time. You wind up your motivational speech and tell the students that it's time to apply what you've taught in their own writing. You try to make it sound like they're standing on the precipice of greatness as writers. They look skeptical. Most stare at their writer's notebooks. You dig in to confer with a student, and there is *so much* work to be done in their writing—you're overwhelmed and don't know where to begin. Fifteen minutes later, you look up and realize that the literacy block is nearly over. No time to share writing today. OK, you really will get that in tomorrow.

You walk the students to lunch feeling that neither you nor the students accomplished nearly as much as any of you would have liked. You feel the frustration bubble up. The time is simply too short to address standards and keep up with the (expletive deleted) district pacing guide, but more importantly, you can't find the time to really dig in, to discuss ideas from their books in more depth, to allow kids to engage in self-chosen writing topics—you need time to confer in a way that differentiates and helps each child set relevant and challenging reading and writing goals. The next day, the process plays out again in exactly the same way. There must be a better way.

> Time has always been a tricky thing in my classroom, but Literacy Studio has helped me use time more efficiently. It has allowed me to take more risks and has made my planning and instruction stronger. I am now not planning separate lessons for reading and writing, but rather thinking how they intertwine in the lesson that I am teaching.
>
> —Karla Contreras, second-grade teacher, Milagro Elementary School, Los Angeles, CA

In your team meeting the next day, you share some of your frustrations.

A team member jumps in immediately. "I know exactly how you feel. Honestly, I feel like I'm planning great writing lessons and I never get to them. By the time I've given kids time to read and conferred with a couple, we're out of time. I just don't know where the time goes."

"It's not just the time—I mean we have two hours; I feel like we spend so much time in test prep writing. 'Read the passage, answer three questions, write an opinion piece about this reading.' It takes so much time," another colleague pops in. "If the two hours were really ours, I'd be able to accomplish so much more. Every once in a while, when I 'let' kids write in their notebooks, they are so excited. I think we could get much better writing from them if they were writing in those notebooks every day—they need practice as writers, just like they need practice as readers—but it's late September, and that's probably happened only two or three times in my class."

Another teacher jumps in. "I hear what you're saying about two hours being enough time, but because we have to have the three reading groups meet each day, I feel like I don't have time to confer with kids and they don't have time to talk to each other about what they're reading and writing. And don't get me started about the pullouts for special ed and interventions. Those kids are coming and going so often I honestly can't keep track. The good news is that the kids who are with me all morning are doing a great job reading and writing for longer and longer periods of time, and they're finally learning how to choose books wisely. But between being caught up in small groups for almost an hour of the block every day and the kids I almost never see because they're out of the classroom, I just don't have time to confer, much less help kids learn to set their own goals."

You interject, "This stuff is all related, the time, the feeling of being boxed into a structure that doesn't allow us to meet kids' needs. Is that really a reader's and writer's workshop at all? I don't mean to sound like I don't have a lot to learn, but I honestly think I could be more responsive to individual needs if we weren't pinned down by the test prep, the groups, the pacing guide, and so on. I want my kids to be challenged, and I get the importance of shooting toward ambitious standards; we just have too many 'have-tos' to feel really effective."

A fourth teacher leans in. "I'm seeing this from a slightly different angle. We do have great conversations about books in my classroom, and I really am trying to use mentor texts to show what great writers do. The kids are amazing in discussions! They have the freshest, most original ideas when we're talking about books. But when it comes time to write in response to a text, or write their own stuff, I'm just getting nothing. Here's the thing. They're writing in the ways we're asking them to. When I tell them they must have a claim and give three kinds of evidence on an assignment, they do it. But, ugh, it's just not even close to the great things they say in discussions. Frankly it's dull, and you get what you ask for. I think the *way* we're asking them to read and write is the culprit. I think I could get them further through conferences where they set their own goals, but as it is, it's getting harder and harder to get them engaged."

Taking Workshop Teaching and Learning to the Next Level

Could that discussion happen among you and your colleagues? It's time to experiment with ways to take workshop teaching (you'll find a brief history later in this chapter) to the next level. It's true that reader's and writer's workshop has provided the space for millions of children to find their identities as readers and writers. Carefully crafted workshops have offered opportunities for authenticity and engagement and, most importantly, time to read and write. There is no question that we need to continue the great work that thousands of teachers and professional authors have brought to the field. And . . .

The teachers whose conversation I excerpted previously are pros. They have years of experience, they are beyond dedicated to their students, they are avid readers of professional texts, and they not only attend great professional development on literacy but also *provide* it for colleagues. But they hadn't fully considered one approach that might be most effective in solving these problems—integrating reading and writing. These teachers had attended elementary schools in which reading and writing were taught separately; they had learned to teach reading and writing separately in preservice training and graduate school; their state standards separate reading and writing; their district's curricula were written by different committees and at different times for reading and writing; in a couple of cases their schedules had lunch, specials, and recess in the middle of the literacy block, which led to reading and writing being taught at two different times in the day; and the upper grades at their school were departmentalized—kids had different teachers for reading and writing. Every possible structure and experience suggested that reading and writing were separate subjects. I've found that is true for most elementary teachers in this country.

I remember my first professional learning centered around Literacy Studio. I left feeling so frustrated, how the heck was I going to integrate reading and writing? It just made no sense to me. I was almost hostile to the idea. Growing up, I learned reading, and then I learned writing. My own learning influenced my teaching. After many conversations with my instructional coach, I decided that it was time to rip off the bandage. I jumped feetfirst into the deep end, and my classroom hasn't been the same since. I started by giving students choice. The simple act of giving students the power to decide for themselves whether they were working on reading or writing brought about immediate changes. My students were more engaged, there was less off-task behavior and their stamina increased, often dramatically. In addition, my conferences became more targeted and in turn, more beneficial to my students.

—Andrew Wallenberg, fifth-grade teacher, Fire Prairie Upper Elementary,
    Fort Osage, MO

I threw out the possibility that several of the most pressing issues the teachers discussed might be mitigated by integrating reading and writing instruction and that really, none of the obstacles I just enumerated were going to make it impossible to do that. In departmentalized settings, collaboration between teachers must be a high priority, but lunch and recess in the middle of the literacy block? No problemo! Separate curricula and standards? We can easily find the connecting points. I told them the story of the year with no snow and my brash remake. I told them how much my kids had contributed to the new design and how much more time and flexibility I had uncovered when I began to integrate reading and writing systematically in the Literacy Studio. You're hearing from some of those teachers throughout this book.

They have gone on to create Literacy Studios in their classrooms; some jumped into the deep end, others took on one component at a time, and each has put their own imprint on their studio. They make revisions, they tweak, they still get frustrated; hey, it's teaching, right? But their kids have more time to read and write. They have more time to confer and otherwise differentiate. Importantly, what their kids learn as readers impacts their writing; what they learn as writers influences the way they read. Now their district has prioritized Literacy Studio K–5, and I stand back and watch them use innovative approaches I couldn't conceive when I first thought about integrating reading and writing. It's amazing to be a part of this kind of change, and it's starting to blossom all over the country.

I should say a word or two about the districts and schools in which I'm privileged to work. My priority, since leaving the classroom, has been to work in high-poverty schools in rural, small urban, and large urban districts. In the early 2000s I was the associate director of a project known as Cornerstone, based at the University of Pennsylvania, in which we provided professional learning opportunities to teachers in several dozen extremely high-poverty schools around the country. I wrote about our work in *To Understand: New Horizons in Reading Comprehension* (2008). Although I have not worked exclusively in high-poverty districts and schools that serve marginalized populations, I have made a personal commitment to prioritize such schools. My greatest joy in this profession comes in being a part of students' lives when they discover their extraordinary intellectual potential and their capacity for impacting social change. Some of my greatest challenges have arisen when I come face-to-face with those who don't believe, for a wide variety of reasons, that all students can learn at high levels. The voice in my head reverberates with, "Wanna *bet*?"

I've been careful in this book to describe *only* schools that serve children of color and/or are situated in high-poverty areas. These schools are in downtown Los Angeles (many of the photos in this book come from this school) and Palmetto, Florida; Fort Osage, Missouri; and Grand Rapids, Michigan, to name a few. Their racial populations differ; some are predominantly Black, others largely Latinx, others very diverse, but in each case, I am honored to work side by side with teachers and principals who have discovered the power of immersing children in rich, diverse texts; of giving them choice in what to write about; in trusting that they can and will think at high levels and probe ideas in discussion and writing and yes, in integrating reading and writing. These are colleagues who personify no-limits learning. They are as indefatigable and brilliant as their students. It is my privilege to bring their stories into this book.

Reader's and Writer's Workshop: A Short History

To get started, it's important to take a quick historical scan to the genesis of reader's and writer's workshop. The work of "workshop" began in writing. Graves (1983) originally described three foundational components of writer's workshop: *time*, *choice or ownership*, and *response*; later the addition of *community* made four. Graves and others, including Hansen (2001) and Bomer and Arens (2020), argued that if we put those four foundational elements in place, students would become more skilled writers and would engage deeply in meaningful, authentic work. I'll discuss time, ownership, response, and community only briefly here—so many others have explored the components in depth and so brilliantly. If you're relatively new to workshop, the online resource Essential Conditions for Literacy Studio (see page ix for access instructions) will give you much more detail about what the four components look like in the classroom. These are the *conditions* that have always been essential for reader's and writer's workshop and remain so for the Literacy Studio.

If we agree that time, ownership, response, and community are the key foundational elements in a workshop or studio, let's reflect on the teachers' conversation earlier. They are looking for a way to give their students more *time* to read and write, more *choice* in the topics and books in which they engage, and the opportunity, as teachers, to *respond* to kids, to differentiate for them through conferences and some small groups. They want their students to engage in a community of readers and writers fully and deeply. I'm guessing that's what you want as well.

How can these teachers, how can you, more thoroughly weave these critical components into your literacy work? Let's begin by refining our understanding of the workshop components because they are also foundations for the Literacy Studio. I will briefly describe each of the components, and I will point out some of the stumbling blocks I've experienced and those other teachers have described to me.

Foundational Components of the Reader's and Writer's Workshop

Time

Do you recall the (perhaps too rare) moments in your classroom when you surveyed the students to see that everyone (OK, nearly everyone) was lost in the experience of reading and writing? You noticed how their gaze fell so intently on the paper or screen in front of them. You wondered if they would have heard the fire alarm if it sounded at that moment! They were feeling the luxury of time. They were released from the anxiety (I chose that word carefully) of wondering when the timer was going to go off, wondering when they would have to move on to another activity, wondering when the startling jolt of an adult voice would say that their time to read and write was over, for now. As their teacher, you may have been acutely aware of the clock and the next big move they must make, to lunch, to music, to math, but you wanted them to be blissfully unaware of those minutes ticking by. You wanted them to feel that they had all the time they needed. That kind of time leads to the engagement we all want for our students (Keene 2018).

We have decades of research and practice (Allington 2011; Ivey and Johnston 2013; Miller and Moss 2013; Harvey et al. 2021) that suggest that students who read *a lot* for significant periods of time each day develop a habit of reading, a joy in doing so, and achieve more on a wide variety of measures. The Ivey and Johnston study, and the other studies it synthesizes, provides the clearest evidence related to each of the foundational elements of reader's and writer's workshop by taking a direct look at engagement during reading and noting the relationship between engagement and achievement.

There are a wide range of other studies with similar conclusions. Read this sentence (if you dare):

> A stepwise multiple regression analysis, in which standardized reading comprehension scores prior to the study served as a covariate, revealed that amount of time spent on reading during the reading period contributed significantly to gains in students' reading achievement. (Taylor, Frye, and Maruyama 1990)

Once we get past the multiple regression analysis, we realize that we have had data *for decades* showing how important it is for students to read for long and growing periods of time. Donald Graves showed the same was true for writing—he published his seminal book, *Writing: Teachers and Children at Work*, in 1983. Writers get better through—hang on for a shocker—writing! It's practice, isn't it? It's common sense.

It comes as a galloping surprise to no one that engagement wanes, or never begins, when kids settle in to read or write and are interrupted six min-

utes later to move on to a new task. So why, going back to the all-too-familiar group of teachers you met at the beginning of this chapter, do we have such difficulty finding the time for students to read and write independently for long and growing periods of time each day?

It's important to know that by helping students build gradually toward longer periods of time spent reading and writing, I do not mean unguided, change-your-book-or-topic-every-three-minutes, spend half-of-the-time-sharpening-

your-pencil, time. The time students spend reading and writing in class is a joyful, engaged time, but they are also hard at work. They are working to apply what your class community has been learning together; they are working on individual goals you've set with them in conferences or small groups; they're monitoring meaning as they read and write, frequently rereading or revising; they're working, but joyfully.

Too many critics of reader's and writer's workshop have characterized workshop as a free-for-all where kids are reading and writing without instruction. In their book *No More Independent Reading Without Support* (2013), Debbie Miller and Barbara Moss are emphatic about the need for explicit instruction in the workshop. The difference, they argue, between DEAR (drop everything and read)-type approaches and true reader's workshop is the instruction and support that lead to ambitious goals toward which students are working during the independent reading time. The same is true for writing. A writer's notebook (Fletcher n.d.) is the home for writing practice. We want to offer choice when kids are practicing in notebooks, it's true, but notebooks are a setting for experimenting with the writer's tools they're learning about.

The bottom line, an argument you scarcely need me to make, is that kids need to build gradually toward extended periods of time each day to read and write. Volume matters. Time engaged in language matters.

Choice/Ownership

As any parent or teacher recalls (or is living through), there is a stage when toddlers and early school-age children insist upon reading a book over and over and over and over. When my own daughter was three, her book of choice was *Moo, Baa, La La La!* by Sandra Boynton. It was "her" book, the one she wanted to hear night after night until her father and I heard "moo, baa, la la la!" in our sleep! She had total control and excelled in using it. It was simply going to be that book. We tried to bring other titles into the nightly routine, but Moo (as she referred to it) was always going to be on the reading list. She found it hilarious. I marvel at how very young children develop such strong preferences and choices. It makes sense though, doesn't it? Their brains are acquiring and developing language at a stunning rate during those stages. Repetition is important to subsequent language use, and they have made their choices and they're sticking with them.

Researchers have made clear that, though the reasons may be different, students of all ages, and adults like you for heaven's sake, need—no, I'll say *demand*—choice in what they read and write about. It simply isn't tolerable to be told, most of the time, what you're going to read and write about. We know, for instance (Keene 2018; Ivey and Johnston 2013), that choice is one of the key correlative factors in student engagement. We simply can't complain about a lack of student engagement if they aren't given a great deal of choice in what they read and write.

That said, engaged students don't always have choice. Think for a moment about the great student discourse that springs from reading the same compelling text. I wouldn't want to say that students never read the same (short) text. Picture books, essays, short nonfiction pieces, art, and photography can all build interest and background knowledge for students, and they love to engage in conversation and perspective bending (Keene 2018) after hearing or reading those texts. We also need to invite students to write across a variety of genres to (a) find the genre that best aligns with their purpose as writers and (b) learn about the almost unlimited ways that they can use their writing to appeal to readers. A strong reader's and writer's workshop depends on choice but is not beholden to choice. What's the balance? Each teacher must decide, but the majority of students' independent reading and writing time should be based on what they choose to read and write.

We also know from teachers like those I quoted at the beginning of this chapter that an enormous amount of work goes into *teaching through modeling* how to choose a great writing topic and how to choose a book that is simultaneously challenging and interesting. It is essential that classroom and school libraries include a wide range of books that serve as mirrors (I can see myself in this book) and windows (I gain insight into others in this book) and sliding glass doors (Bishop 1990) (I can walk into the world of those represented in the book). Students are invited to choose from a large, diverse, and growing classroom library. Books by Black, Latinx, Indigenous, and other people of color should be amplified during read-alouds so that students make subsequent choices to read them again and write about topics raised in them. It is also vital that students are encouraged to choose a range of topics and genre in which they can experiment as writers.

In their study, Ivey and Johnston (2013) asked eighth-grade *students* (imagine that) about the impact of choice in what they read and its relationship to their engagement. The kids told them in no uncertain terms what they needed to be engaged. "As *causal factors* [emphasis added], not outcomes, the students also identified time to read, choice, teacher behavior, and books. Time to read and choice were singular and specific." Like our toddlers and primary-grade students, it seems that readers and writers throughout the age continuum need choice to engage. As Ivey and Johnston write, it's a causal connection. Engagement (Guthrie and Wigfield 2000), as we have known for two decades, leads to improved reading achievement.

Response

Student Discourse

In my own classroom, once students had settled into a routine, I set aside time each day for one book club to meet. They had selected a novel from a collection I narrowed down for them and read a certain number of pages each week. I created discussion questions and sat in on each book club to ensure that students stayed focused on the book. I'd give anything to have those moments back, to get out of their way, to open the discussions to what they noticed, what confounded them, what others thought. Even though I needed too much control and therefore botched the infrastructure for book clubs in my classroom, my kids clamored for them. They couldn't wait for their book club day, and I'd catch snatches of conversations throughout the week. "Did you get to the part where . . ." When the day rolled around, though, I noticed that students' responses were often limp attempts to answer my discussion questions and that the student discussion I noticed *outside* the book club was more animated than when we were seated around the table. They were dying to talk to each other about books; their teacher was in the way.

I needn't have been worried about kids working on their own. Ivey and Johnston noted, "Students in this study, when fully engaged, were not disrupted by conversations among other students and preferred to be able to solicit conversation at the point of need, developing strategies for soliciting conversations only from willing peers" (2013, 272). In other words, students could have productive conversations without the heavy-handed structures I had used, but I wasn't alone.

Interestingly, the Ivey and Johnston study noted that "the data also indicate that socially meaningful talk and active listening lead to a sense of relatedness and of feeling appreciated and understood by others including teachers" (2013, 271). Ivey and Johnston cite Reis and colleagues as corroborating evidence: "As students became more engaged with one another and with characters in the books in self-generated discussions, they encountered others and themselves differently and had an altered sense of the significance of difference" (2000, 270).

Conferences and Other Forms of Discourse Between Students and Teachers

It's hard to overstate the importance of talk in literacy classrooms. In *Writing: Teachers and Children at Work* (1983), Donald Graves highlighted writing conferences with individual students as a way to hone teacher feedback related to class goals and student needs. He saw conferences as an opportunity to listen deeply and carefully to students' intentions in their writing: What is this child trying to do with this piece? What tools can I provide right now that will help them move forward as a writer? We have since learned that conferring is perhaps the most potent way to differentiate for writers *and* readers.

We know from research that students learn best with a combination of guided practice and opportunities to practice independently (Rosenshine 1995). Conferences provide the most tailored possible response to students' reading and writing in the moment. In a conference the teacher and student work together to analyze the student's use of a current class objective and on that student's individual goals, what we'll call intentions (often set by the student in collaboration with the teacher).

Most teachers have moved away from the red pen form of feedback most of us endured as developing writers and have moved, very productively, toward writing conferences. We fully understand that students need to focus on the new moves they're making in a piece of writing; they need to keep their audience and purpose in mind and have autonomy in choosing how to craft their pieces. They need to be collectors (in notebooks) of ideas for potential pieces, and they need to be wide awake to the world around them to fill those notebooks with original observations and insights. We want to respond to students' writing (and reading) by asking questions about their intent and their purpose, and then we need to listen. Conferring may be one of the most difficult teaching moves we make—we're unsure about what to say in some situations; we're tempted to overwhelm a child with advice; we notice everything "wrong" with a student's writing as opposed to finding the "gems" (Bomer 2010) to develop into strong pieces, rich with children's voices.

Reading conferences are just as important and rely on many of the same principles and teaching moves. In his book *Conferring: The Keystone of the Reader's Workshop*, Patrick Allen (2009) advocates for three distinct components for a reading conference, which he shortens to RIP. The *R* stands for review, read aloud, and record; the *I* for instruction, insights, and intrigue; and the *P* for plan, progress, and purpose. Essentially, Patrick suggests that, like in writing conferences, we take a few moments to think about the child's progress since we last met, perhaps ask the child to read aloud, and reflect on their progress toward goals set at the previous conference. In the second phase of the conference, we engage with the student in discussion about what they would like to tackle next, providing the instruction necessary for them to move ahead; and finally, in the third phase, we set goals and send them off to work. The teacher is in a collaborative role throughout, and we allow ourselves to be intrigued (my favorite verb that Patrick uses) by what we're learning from the child and thinking with them about what they might try next as a reader.

Of course, conferences aren't the only type of verbal interaction (response) we have with students. We have untold thousands of interactions with students each year. In *Talk About Understanding* (Keene 2012), I laid out the Talk About Understanding principles, a short list (see Figure 2.1) that we can keep in mind when we're interacting with groups and individuals.

Talk About Understanding Principles

Ten Ways to Modify Language to Enhance Understanding

To enhance understanding when teaching or talking informally to students, we should:

1. **Vary the tone of our speech—speak in the quietest tone** appropriate for the situation; garner children's attention by speaking more quietly, not more forcefully.

2. **Vary the pace** of our talk depending on the context and the content.

3. **Vary the intensity and expression of emotion** we use verbally and nonverbally to reveal which concepts and ideas are most essential for children to understand and remember.

4. **Use sophisticated vocabulary** but define the words in the context of the discussion; use these words repeatedly.

5. **Speak with heightened civility and respect,** making clear the distinction between settings in which informal language is appropriate and the need for more formal, academic language in other learning situations.

Figure 2.1 Talk About Understanding Principles   *continues*

To enhance understanding when we're responding to children's talk, we should:

6. **Use silence** frequently, giving students an opportunity to think about concepts; serve as a model for taking time to think.

7. **Restate and probe** children's responses during discussions, giving them a chance to further reflect on what they have said and to probe ideas further.

8. **Label children's ideas with language we want all children to use**; display the language your community uses to describe thinking and use the same language consistently across the content areas.

9. **Use a variety of syntax**—vary the length of sentences, depending on the purpose and content of instruction; expand what children are saying into more fully developed sentences without changing the central ideas they are trying to communicate.

10. **Facilitate the transition from one child's comment to a larger spirited and informed discussion about ideas**; show passion, surprise and moments of insight about ideas; model what it means to **consider the perspectives of others in conversation** and revise one's knowledge and beliefs because of those perspectives.

Figure 2.1 Talk About Understanding Principles, *continued*

We all strive to provide responses that build agency, ignite engagement, and encourage more thoughtful reading and writing. We know the importance of guiding students' practice. The difficulty, as you heard from the teachers at the beginning of the chapter, is finding the time to tailor our responses to each student's needs.

Community

Perhaps the most intangible component of a great reader's and writer's workshop is *community*; many of the elements in a healthy, supportive workshop community are invisible and inaudible but essential to the adventure that is learning to read and write. As I mentioned earlier in this chapter, I have compiled an extensive list of the conditions present when we seek a close-knit classroom community. You can find it online (see page ix for access instructions). I'll briefly summarize some of those conditions here, but suffice to say that these conditions warrant a book in and of themselves.

It is important to begin our conversation about classroom community with some thoughts about the school as a whole. We create our classroom communities within the larger context of school and district policies and curricula, state and national policies, our leaders' knowledge base, and, importantly, our own and others' beliefs about children's learning. These beliefs are often expressed in the shorthand language we use to describe students: she's a special ed kid, they move a lot, he really struggles, they have a tough home life, they are disruptive. If the goals for our classrooms include building empathy, promoting equity, and embracing students from every background, we must begin by interrogating our own biases—uncovering ways in which we project racism, classism, or sexism without being fully aware of it. I have begun this work and will continue to do so throughout my life. I have learned about systemic racism, for example, by reading and confronting it in the workplace. I have been silent when I should have spoken. I know that I, in fact all of us, need to look at ourselves in the mirror and ask if we believe, in our heart of hearts, that all children can learn at high levels and contribute meaningfully to social change. And where there is a seed of doubt, we need to wrestle with it until

> *If the goals for our classrooms include building empathy, promoting equity, and embracing students from every background, we must begin by interrogating our own biases—uncovering ways in which we project racism, classism, or sexism without being fully aware of it.*

it is no longer a part of our beliefs. We must work to check ourselves at the slightest hint of "kid blaming" or "family blaming." We need to project an asset-based view of children rather than describing students by labels inflicted upon them. We need to develop trust in ourselves and to speak out in conversations in which a deficit view of children is expressed; we can and should take responsibility for building a habit of professional discourse in which diversity, equity, and inclusion is valued and *acted upon*. Each of these elements of self-examination is essential if we are to serve every child with the respect they deserve.

Within our classrooms, respect for children and their work simply permeates every interaction—those among children and those between children and teachers—and we know it when we see and hear it. The teacher sets the tone. As I describe in Essential Conditions for Literacy Studio (available online), we work to create a classroom atmosphere that communicates that "we're all in this together" and that there is no perfect, complete learner; it is the work of a lifetime to use language effectively and explore ideas, and adults are working just as hard as children to do so. The teacher serves as lead learner, modeling how learners live in the world and speaking frequently and openly about interests, frustrations, successes, routines, and rituals, encouraging children to take risks as thinkers. Teachers show that to be engaged is to embrace struggle and revel in the joy of working through difficult problems. There is a pervasive impression of pride in the precious space and the people within it and clarity about how people mutually care for a space closely shared with others.

In a workshop community, children share their ideas, not for the sake of sharing but because they believe others will benefit. They prepare themselves to discuss complex topics that are current and relevant to their own and others' lives outside school. When pursuing topics as researchers, they consider the implications of their findings in the social and natural world. They are attuned to other's needs, feel empathy, and act in and out of school settings to mitigate conflict in the world.

Creating a community that supports avid, engaged learning is essential to your reader's and writer's workshop and will be essential to your Literacy Studio. Doing so requires experience, mindfulness, and feedback from your colleagues and leaders.

These four components are the underpinnings for your Literacy Studio just as they are if you currently teach in a reader's and writer's workshop. It can feel overwhelming though. How do we know if we have the important conditions in place for optimal language learning? Consider this as a starting place—spend a few minutes writing off the well-known prompt "This I Believe" and focus your writing on the elements you believe are crucial in building the components of time, ownership, response, and community you know best support readers and writers. Post your belief statement, as Debbie Miller taught me to do, above your workspace. Refer to it often, think about your "lines in the sand"—your beliefs about children for which you are willing to stand up and speak out, question and challenge, though it may be quite uncomfortable to do so. As teachers, we must be mindful about the moral and ethical imperatives that drive our work. Those imperatives are alive and well inside you, and they will provide the foundation for your Literacy Studio.

Ask any teacher what they need more of, and you'll get the same answer over and over: **time**. Literacy Studio has given this advantage to teachers. The framework has slowed down time for our teachers, or more precisely, it has created the illusion of more time. Integrating reading and writing into one joint lesson, and focusing on what's most important, deeply, over a significant span of time has been key to our teachers feeling empowered to dig deeper with students, to linger instead of jumping from one standard to another.

—Erica Wood, Instructional Coach, Fire Prairie Upper Elementary, Fort Osage, MO

The teachers whose conversation I summarized earlier in this chapter made the transition from reader's and writer's workshop to Literacy Studio to resolve some of the issues that plagued them and their students. They started by writing their belief statements and talking about which of their current practices aligned with their beliefs and which did not. Those practices were eliminated or minimized. They focused on weaving reading and writing instruction into a single whole- or small-group lesson, they gave kids much more choice, and they altered their planning processes (see Chapter 3), all of which netted more time for students to read and write and much more engagement. They continue to this day to refine their practices as literacy teachers and to share what they've discovered with colleagues around the country.

In today's literacy world, packaged and scripted programs proliferate and often lead teachers down paths to separate instruction in reading and writing. Isolated reading and writing and teacher- or program-driven concepts are the norm; students rarely set their own goals and are lucky if they have choice in what to read and write, let alone when to read and when to write. Too often, students experience diminished engagement and teachers *feel* that something is just not right; it's not the workshop they envision for their children.

Reader's and writer's workshop is and was always meant to be driven by students' needs and interests with a skilled teacher at their side. Reader's and writer's workshops have served us well for many years, and the foundational elements of time, ownership, and response are just as important today. And . . .

And we are ready to take the next step. We can build on the tremendous successes of workshop teaching, arguably one of the most significant pedagogical changes in American public schooling, and welcome students into twenty-first-century learning. Our teaching world has changed. There are demands on us that the founding parents of workshop never imagined. And we've learned so much from nearly forty years of workshop teaching. Brilliant educators around the world have refined and reimagined both reader's and writer's workshops, and we continue to learn and rethink. Literacy Studio is the product of that rethinking, so let's dive in!

CHAPTER THREE

It's All About the Planning!

As a teacher at the elementary and university level, I was an obsessive planner. I was determined to write down every possible variation a lesson might take; I wanted to be prepared for anything a student might say or do, every eventuality. Picture my plans as a flowchart—if this, then that; if that, then this—arrows and all. I did not want surprise. In fact, I was terrified of surprise. What if a student asked a question to which I did not know the answer? Little did I know that those questions would become the ones I cherish the most. I awoke many times in the middle of the night, on my sofa, papers and plans strewn around me, still in my work clothes, not finished with my elaborate plans for the next day and desperate for sleep. Weren't we just so tired in those first few years?! So tired. And I never felt fully prepared. As I drove to school, I ran through each block of time in my head.

To imagine that, eventually, my go-to planning document would be a simple, one-page tool that could include everything I needed to know for a day, or a week, was beyond me in those years. But simplicity is often where true genius lies, and I owe my dear friend and colleague Debbie Miller all the credit.

The Planning Wheel: A Tool to Integrate Reading and Writing

Several years ago, Debbie and I were sitting in the gate area waiting for our flight to Kansas City where we would be working with teachers for a few days. I don't remember the context of the conversation, but I do remember that Debbie opened her notebook, which was covered with notes and arrows connecting one idea to another (not unlike my early lesson planning, but far more organized, full of colorful charts and categories for her most recent thinking and lesson plans). She's a planning *artist*. She flipped to a page to show me a planning tool that she and Samantha Bennett (2007) had created. It's a pie chart (you'll see my revision in Figure 3.1 on page 38) and has three main sections for planning notes. Debbie and Sam had created the tool for reader's workshop, adding the portion at the top that lists the learning target and a space to describe the evidence of student learning we hope to see at the end of the lesson. It had been useful, she told me, for capturing everything you want to happen in a lesson on a single, easy-to-use page and it helped prioritize what matters most in the workshop—time for students to do the real work of reading and writing. Everything is right in front of you.

> Starting Literacy Studio was a bit tricky because I was overthinking and was being very rigid. I think it was more of a need for control for myself and changing the way that I teach is scary. The uncertainty is extremely hard to embrace, even though we preach it to students. Students eagerly welcomed the change and loved being able to choose what would help them grow that day.
>
> —Karla Contreras, second-grade teacher, Milagro Elementary School, Los Angeles, CA

Another true confession: I have a serious problem with time. Once I'm in a classroom surrounded by children and we're reading, thinking aloud, discussing the ideas in a book, I can go on forever. If the kids are engaged, I *choose* to ignore the clock, lose myself in the conversation, and end up sacrificing time for the students to read and write independently. I won't ask you to raise your hand if you do this, but I'm pretty sure I'm not the only one! It's just *so much fun* to talk about books and writing, and when students are leaning into the conversation to share their original ideas . . . well, I could stay all day and into the night. So, for me, planning and sticking to the plan is essential. Debbie's planning wheel, which I've revised in Figure 3.1, has saved me. I want to describe in detail how I use it, but before I do, let's define some terms that we'll use throughout the book.

Learning target: A concept, strategy, standard, curriculum objective, or tool—literacy content—on which the teacher provides instruction. Learning targets are written into plans (see Figure 3.1 on page 38) but may be revised based on students' demonstrated needs. The teacher expects students to show evidence of their application of the learning target when it is appropriate in the context of their reading and writing.

Evidence: Student work that shows they have applied the strategies and/or tools that have been taught. This evidence may be written, oral, artistic, or dramatic and is often in the form of the student's daily notebook writing, recording thinking about text they read, and/or conversation with other readers and writers. Evidence may include but does not imply a formal assessment and may be graded. The teacher and student look at some evidence together and talk about the student's progress over time.

Strategy: The learning targets (content) we teach that extend *beyond* what students will use in any one text or piece of writing. For example, when we help writers *elaborate* key ideas in their writing, we are teaching them a strategy that can be used in nearly any writing they do. When we teach thinking strategies such as *monitoring for meaning, determining importance, inferring,* we are teaching students to use a thinking strategy that applies more broadly than a single text.

Tool: Content we have taught that is specific to certain individual texts, writing pieces, or genres. For example, we might help a student use dialogue to describe a character and ask them to study dialogue in a particular book to understand more about a character. These are tools that are useful in certain texts, contexts, and genres. The use of white space and line breaks in poetry is a tool readers and writers can use in poetry; a narrative writer introduces internal and external conflict; a nonfiction reader and writer manipulate certain text features such as bold, italics, and so on.

Goals: Suggestions (or requests) that a teacher makes to encourage a student to try a new concept in their reading and/or writing. Goals may stem from review of students' work or instruction in Crafting Sessions or Invitational Groups; they relate to what we want students to apply independently. Ideally, our goals are supplemented or replaced by students' intentions as the year goes on.

Goals may or may not be immediately applicable to reading and writing the student is doing. The teacher keeps track (on Google Docs, anchor charts, or class thinking notebooks or in other accessible ways) of new learning; all students should apply what is taught when it is relevant to their reading and writing (unless they already demonstrate the use of the tool or strategy). Goals should, whenever possible, align with the students' intentions.

Intentions: What the student is trying to work on as a reader and writer in a text or written piece; the impact they are working to create in their writing or the ways they are working to understand more deeply in their reading. Intentions can be short or long term—something they want to accomplish in a particular text or piece of writing or ways in which they want to change their identity and habits as a reader or writer.

Note: A goal and an intention can be the same thing if the student and teacher agree that the student wants to give something new a try.

Back to the planning wheel. When I saw the planning wheel Debbie used, I was immediately drawn to it to keep my time problem under control. Take another look at Figure 3.1 on page 38. Debbie explained.

1. First (top of planning wheel), think about your learning target, the standard, objective, curriculum focus. What content do you want your students to discuss and apply? Then ask yourself this question: "Is the target important or worthy of their time?" Generally speaking, we are trying to teach way too much, sacrificing depth for coverage. Don't be afraid to go in greater depth on fewer learning targets. Students will retain and reapply better if you are more focused and providing depth in your instruction.

2. Then, start planning with the biggest chunk of time (12:00–8:00 position if we look at the planning wheel as a clock), *children's independent work*—known in the Literacy Studio as Composing, which includes their reading, writing, and planned or spontaneous interactions with each other. Students will spend most of this time reading and writing. Pure and simple. When completing this part of the plan, consider questions like these: What do you envision for the independent composing time? What would composing look like on the *best* day? What's your ideal? Then ask: What learning goal do you want students to try, to experiment with as readers or writers? What do you want them to apply from your recent instruction? What individual intentions or class goals are the children working on? Are students reading books and writing on topics that are engaging to them? There may be other learning work you'd like for them to engage in with partners or self-directed small groups during this time. What might that look like? We need to ensure that these learning activities don't take too much time away from the actual work of reading and writing, but we can consider questions like these: In what ways might students experiment with their learning target/goal in pairs before they try it on their own? How will kids interact with each other during this, the largest chunk of time in the Studio time? Do you need to see small needs-based groups during this time? I answer all these questions in the largest space, labeled *Composing*. I also use this space to jot the names of students with whom I want to confer that week.

3. The next step is to complete the evidence space (at the top of the form). Now that you know the learning target and have imagined the work students will do, what learning evidence do you hope to see during and after the students' independent work time? Remember, evidence doesn't mean a pen-and-paper assessment. Evidence can be as simple as collecting students' sticky notes or as complex as a written response to

text they've been working on for several days. It may be some visible or audible outcome or evidence of a student's thinking that you discover and note during a conference.

4. There's another important component to consider, also found at the top of the form, the strategy. In that space, the teacher asks this important question: What *thinking* do students need to do to be successful in working toward the learning target? For example, if the learning target relates to identifying key ideas and evidence, determining importance is one of the thinking strategies that will help students apply the learning target. Learning targets almost always connect to a thinking strategy, and the strategy will apply in whatever book students are reading and whatever they are writing, beginning now and into their future work, whereas the learning target, key ideas, and evidence in this example won't apply to everything they read and write. To work toward this long-term retention and reapplication, we must consider the types of thinking they need to do and connect the strategies to learning targets such as standards and curriculum. Otherwise, the learning target becomes a one-day experience applied in one book or one piece of writing. If the learning is contextualized in a thinking strategy, however, it has staying power. By definition, a strategy can be applied by readers and writers in nearly everything they read and write. We'll explore this concept much more in the coming chapters, but for now consider the comprehension thinking strategies we described in *Mosaic of Thought* (Keene and Zimmermann 2007). Will the students need to generate questions, determine what's important, add to their schema, infer, create images, synthesize, or monitor meaning closely? I suggest incorporating the one or two thinking strategies most relevant to the learning target, but don't worry too much about picking "the right one." Thinking strategies are useful in nearly every literacy learning experience.

5. Now, after you've thought about goals, how students will spend their independent work time, the evidence you'll look for, and the thinking they'll learn to do, go back and look at the portion that indicates what you'll focus on in your large-group instruction time (the portion in the 8:30–12:00 position). That's the time for whole-group instruction or occasionally small-group instruction. There you can make notes about how you want to teach into the learning target, what texts and writing samples (your own or kids') you might use, what you'd like to think aloud about during the short time (we'll talk about how short in Chapter 4) you're with children as a large group; the time when you pique their interest about engaging in something new as readers and writers, the time when you say, "You're so ready, go out and try it!" This large community time is known as the *Crafting Session*.

6. Finally, think about the slice of time from about 8:00 to 8:30 on the planning wheel. That's the time for reflecting on how the independent work, the Composing, went that day. It's largely focused on kids sharing different things they tried as readers and what they intend to do the next day to deepen their application of the learning target and thinking strategy. When you complete this section, consider: What kind of reflection (whole group, pair sharing, etc.) is the best fit for the learning target and the work they've done? How can you gather evidence of their progress? Reflection time is an important way to tie everything together from the lesson, the independent work and other learning targets that relate to this work in some way. Students should always relate their learning to the larger world—how the learning target, and especially the thinking strategy, will help them beyond the work of the day, into the wider school and world community.

I thought (and still do) that this simple planning tool was a work of genius. In simplicity is often found the greatest elegance (that's a quote from my mom—I didn't get what she was talking about when I was a kid, but I do now). I saw some ways that I wanted to adapt it and, with Debbie's permission, did exactly that. I added the portion related to the thinking strategy(ies) that will be important for students to meet the learning target. Later I made additional adaptations, which I'll describe in subsequent chapters of the book. For now, take a look at this simple tool and actually use it to plan an upcoming lesson. Make a quick copy of Appendix 1 and just take it out for a spin! (To download a copy of the planning wheel, please visit http://hein.pub/LitStudio and click on Companion Resources.)

Adaptations for the Planning Wheel

I've found that one circle may work for two or three days of the week—very few learning targets worth the students' attention are accomplished in a day. You may find that you have two or three planning wheels that encompass a week or even two weeks' work. I like to share the planning wheels with the students at the beginning of the day (or just project them on the document camera) so students always have an idea of what's coming next. I use an arrow to show where we'll enter the work that day. (Read on for some adaptations.)

You're probably already thinking about adaptations for the planning wheel—might we start with Reflection from the previous day's work and then go into independent work time, break it in half for a whole-group lesson? Of course, that's why it's a circle! There are dozens of configurations you can imagine for the use of this planning tool. At the beginning of the year, consider using a consistent, predictable order for the first few weeks or a month of school so that the children become used to how Literacy Studio works. Then feel free to mix it up. Ask the kids what order they would like to work in the next day or so.

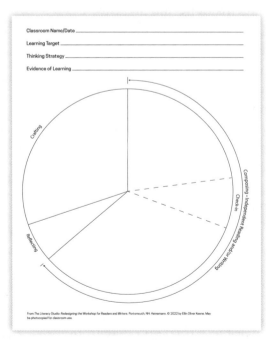

Figure 3.1 Planning Wheel

Figure 3.2 shows a lesson I planned very early in my use of the planning wheel. You can see that I made revisions before the lesson and jotted notes and questions about students with whom I conferred and words I didn't quite finish—it's a real draft. You'll also find the T-chart form I used for the anchor chart and for each child in Figure 3.3.

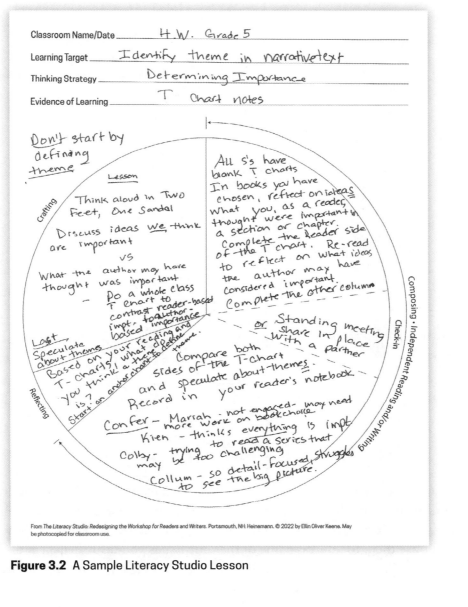

Figure 3.2 A Sample Literacy Studio Lesson

Determining Importance—What Matters Most?

Name _____   Date _____

Ideas I think are most important	Ideas the author thinks are most important

Ideas I think are most important (*continued*)   **Ideas the author thinks are most important** (*continued*)

Additional thinking—why did I make these decisions?

_____

_____

_____

_____

_____

_____

_____

Figure 3.3 Determining Importance—
What Matters Most?

It was so easy and practical and really forced me to prioritize the children's work time. Throughout this book and in the online resources you'll read about many lessons that were born on the planning wheel and get a sense of how we might use them to address some of the time issues you heard teachers discuss at the beginning of Chapter 2. Just keep this simple structure in mind. One sheet, one plan, very straightforward. Or is it?

How Do We Think About Planning in a Literacy Studio Where Our Lessons Are Integrated?

This sample lesson only focuses on reading. What about writing? In the prelude and in Chapters 1 and 2, I argued that we need to focus on integrating writing and reading. Except for the T-charts, there was no writing in the sample lesson. Do we create another planning wheel for writing? Let me take you through my process.

First plan: It came to me on a Sunday evening when (like you) I was writing plans for my work in the coming week. I would be working alongside the teachers at Tillman Elementary in Palmetto, Florida, a school I love. I was completing the planning wheel with a focus on reading when I realized that the learning target—examining character change and the resulting impact on a narrative plot—applied every bit as much to writers as it did to readers.

Why would I create two plans to teach the same thing? Why wouldn't it be possible to teach *one* lesson that incorporated the reader's view *and* the writer's view?

Why couldn't the evidence or application for readers go beyond the mundane sticky note marking of their texts when they noticed character and plot changes? Wouldn't it be better to have them work on an ongoing piece of narrative writing and shape the characters' change to show its impact on plot *in their writing*? The more I thought about it, the more I realized how much sense it made. I could still use the mentor text (I chose *Something Beautiful* by Sharon Dennis Wyeth [2002]); I could still think aloud about how the character's actions shaped the plot; *and* the third graders could show in their own writing how character changes, which are very clear in this lovely story, impact the plot. Then I chickened out. I started to worry about how many of the students would have ongoing narrative pieces, who would be at the beginning stages of such a piece, and which kids would need to read more to fully understand the concept. Too many variables, I decided, especially when I'm not the children's teacher. I tossed out the planning wheel and started again.

Second plan: Back to just reading. I tried to focus only on reading but found that I just couldn't do it. The more I thought about it, the more I was convinced that the lesson shouldn't be simply a reading or a writing lesson. You know the drill; more sticky notes to show character change in your book. Reading lesson. The next day, reread the book to see how the author shows character change—write a short piece in which a character changes. That's the way we often use mentor texts, isn't it? Ugh. I wanted to combine them. I started again. New planning wheel.

Third plan: On my third try, I remembered to start my plan with what I wanted the children to *do* in independent work time. What does the big piece of the pie look like? Easy—I wanted them to read *and* write. As a matter of fact, why couldn't they differentiate for themselves by—hang in there with me—*choosing* whether to read *and/or* write?

Why couldn't third graders decide, following the lesson, what *they* needed to do to work toward understanding how characters' changes impact the plot? We just never ask them! The learning target was the same for everyone, but they could (initially) choose to experiment with the concept as writers or follow the character's changes as readers. They might feel more enthused about trying to show character change in texts they were already writing, or they may want to read their book choice with an eye to character and plot change. Anything wrong with that?

What about my role? When I sat down to confer with a child, I would simply conduct a reading conference if they were engrossed in a book or a writing conference if they were writing. I'd take notes related to the learning target and explore any goals the child may have.

Why have two separate sets of notes for reading and writing conferences?

The Components of Literacy Studio— Briefly Explained

The Lesson (Which We Call the Crafting Session)

In the third grade later that week, I began by only hinting at the choice students would make about whether to read or write. I modeled first by talking about a character in a novel I was reading, *Three Flames* (Lightman 2019). I talked about how her actions were changing the plot as I read. They had a few questions and insights, and, in the discussion, I switched back and forth from the reader's perspective to the writer's perspective. I actually chose a very short, age-appropriate section of the novel to read aloud to them.

Me: You know, as I'm reading this book, I can't help but think about the different choices the mother might have made early in her life and how much it would have changed her children's lives.

I continued reading and paused a few moments later to think aloud from the point of view of a writer.

Me: Do you guys remember that I'm working on a book about my puppies, Charlie and Maggie? (I had shared a portion of it on a previous visit.)

They remembered.

Me: What if I, as the writer, decided to show how the puppies have changed, became less naughty as we trained them? I can show how they now do a lot of sweet, loving things in addition to still doing a few naughty things, like pulling the Christmas tree down.

The students were all over that idea.

Various students: Yeah, because right now it seems like all they do is bad stuff, but they're getting better! I wondered why you didn't train them not to do that stuff! I thought maybe you'd give them away.

(Never!)

Me: So, what if I wrote about how Charlie likes to cuddle even though he is a big basset hound? What if I told you that they're the best vacuum cleaners for crumbs in the world? What if I told you that when we have company, Maggie likes to lie on the visitor's feet? How would my book change then?

As usual, the conversation consumed us as we talked about all the plot possibilities in the novel I was reading and in the outcomes in my book, *The Charlie and Maggie Chronicles*. We literally talked about readers' and writers' perspectives on the learning target right through the lesson time. But instead of pressing on, as if I was compelled to do what I had written on the planning wheel, I stopped.

Reading *Something Beautiful* would have to wait until tomorrow. Because the energy was so high in the room, I would have been missing a huge opportunity not to let the students dig in right then.

The Independent Work Time (Which We Call Composing Time)

Me: OK, you guys.

I lowered my voice significantly and added a dose of drama.

Me: What do you think about this? What if some kids decided to go back into your choice books to follow the character's changes and think about how those changes impact the plot, and other kids continue with or start a narrative piece where you, as the author, make the characters change over time and decide how those changes will affect the plot?

They stared at me. I tried again.

Me: Some of you can choose to read right now and some of you can choose to write.

Student: At the same time?!

Me: Well, you might want to read for a while to focus on character changes and then try it out as a writer. Or you might want to start with writing and manipulate the characters so they change over time, which will impact the events in the story.

They were having a hard time grasping the choice I was offering.

Student: So, some of us will read and other kids will write?

Me: Exactly.

The observing teachers squelched laughter.

Me: So, tell me, who thinks they'll start off by reading?

Hands shot up.

Me: Who thinks they might start by writing?

Surprisingly, more hands went up.

Me: And who isn't sure?

Three hands.

I used a staggered send-off. I sent the children who intended to write off to find their notebooks to get started. The rest of the class watched them as I narrated their movements loudly enough that the writers could hear.

> **Me:** Look, you guys, they're heading off to get their notebooks. They're thinking about the characters they're writing about. If they're just starting a story today, they're thinking about the characters whose stories they want to tell. Now you're going to see them find great writing spots around the classroom. See? I told you! Look at Carlos! You're going to see him open his notebook, and I'll bet he starts to make lists about how his characters might change, or maybe he'll just start writing while thinking about the characters and the plot.

I did the same thing as the readers went off to grab their book boxes. I reminded the three waiting with me what the readers would focus on in their reading that day. Having watched the two groups begin, one boy said, "I'm going to write!" and off he went. He just needed a bit more time. Two remained.

> **Me:** OK, you two. What are you thinking?
>
> **Student:** I don't know what to do, which one to pick.
>
> **Me:** That's not a problem. Why don't we quietly walk around the room and look at what the readers and writers are doing? You just let me know when you've decided what you want to try first. Look, you can always change your mind, right?

They looked genuinely surprised. They could change their minds?! They both ended up reading. It rounded the group off to about half who chose to begin by reading and the other half writing.

I took a moment, as I always try to do, to walk around the room—just to observe. Most were digging in. I narrated my observations aloud, like I was talking to myself.

> **Me:** Oh wow, this is really working. Some kids are reading. Some kids are writing. I bet they're thinking about the characters and how their changes

affect the plot. Wow, these kids are focused. Oh, I do see some kids looking up; I guess they're spending some time thinking.

This was optimistic at best, but it jarred them back to the work at hand.

Check-in

About halfway through the independent work time, I called for a "standing meeting." There are many ways to use a check-in time in the middle of Composing. But in a standing meeting, everyone stops what they're doing and gathers as a large group for a sort of status check. It's a moment to discuss insights and discoveries about their work as readers and writers thus far and to get a sense of what they plan to do next. Everyone stays standing, which permits them to move a bit and, because we're not sitting to discuss something, prevents us from getting too comfortable and going on too long. A standing meeting or any kind of check-in can provide a nice midway point for kids to decide if they're going to continue reading or writing (as they began) or if they're going to make a switch. The overall learning goal remains the same. They're looking for or creating characters who are dynamic, who change over the course of the narrative, resulting in particular outcomes in the events and the overall plot.

After this standing meeting, about ten students decided to switch to reading or writing; in other words, to experiment with the learning target in a way they hadn't tried yet. We'll talk about record keeping a bit later in the book but suffice to say that *they* are doing the record keeping—yes, even kindergartners!

Sharing Time (Which We Call Reflection)

At the end of the independent work time, I asked those who had read for at least part of the time to stand and hold up either their notebook or their book and locate someone who was holding the other. Readers met with writers. Writers met with readers. I asked them to share examples of the learning target (what they tried) from both perspectives—the reader and the writer—with their partners and mentioned that if they started out as a reader today, they would be asked to start out as a writer tomorrow and vice versa, so it was in their best interest to get some tips from others who had experimented in the other form. (The next day, we actually got to the reading of *Something Beautiful*.)

The students shuffled around and found a partner. Of course, some wanted to work with kids who were already with a partner—"Can there be three? I can't find anyone who wrote." I said, "What do you think I might say to that question?" and they replied, "Yes?" I nodded. Some things never change. The first time you try this type of Reflection, it will feel a little chaotic, but students get to the point where they really are seeking and obtaining advice for how to apply the learning target in another mode.

Figure 3.4 shows the planning wheel for the lesson that became two lessons that week.

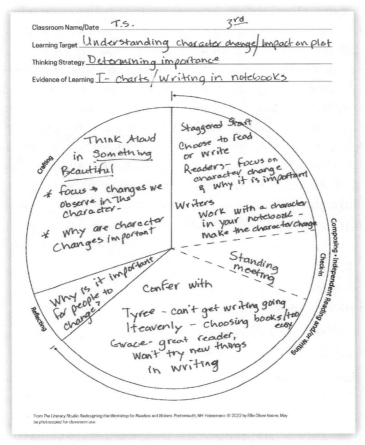

Figure 3.4 Completed Planning Wheel

Planning for the Year

By now you're starting to manage a growing cacophony of questions in your mind: How do the standards and my district's curricula play out in a Literacy Studio? How can I be sure that students are reading and writing with increasing fluency and control? How often do we publish writing in a Literacy Studio? How does a teacher grade students' work? How do English learners fare in a Literacy Studio? I promise we'll address each one of those issues, but given that this is a chapter on planning, I thought it might be helpful to present a yearlong overview for an intermediate and a primary Literacy Studio showing how standards are integrated in the Literacy Studio. You'll notice that, at any given time in the school year, the overarching concept is one or more of the thinking strategies. They provide the essential link between the standards and reading and writing. When focusing on questioning, for example, the standards are taught through the lens of asking questions. Asking questions is the "connective tissue" that helps us tie disparate concepts together and helps us plan for integrated lessons. In Figures 3.5 and 3.6, I provide an outline to show how you might integrate standards, thinking strategies, reading, and writing for the school year. I have only incorporated the Common Core State Standards in reading (informational and narrative) and in writing. Your district may break them down further into curriculum, but you will see how they fit together. Remember that thinking strategies and standards are meant to be woven into instruction throughout the year—they're not a one-and-done proposition. You will continue to revisit standards and thinking strategies throughout the school year; they will be emphasized at times like in the examples in Figures 3.5 and 3.6.

Some important ideas to keep in mind:

- Genre studies may include "subgenre" (i.e., biography, personal narrative, research writing).

- Poetry is not taught as a separate unit—poems, writing and reading, are woven into each week's work with students.

- Students in grades 2 and above keep a writer's notebook throughout the year in which they experiment with concepts they've been taught, topics about which they might be interested, goals as a writer, drafts, and so on. The notebooks are generally paper and pencil but can be digital. (See Chapter 7.)

- Students in kindergarten and first grade compose in little books (see Chapter 7) and on other writing surfaces appropriate to their development as writers.

- Students in all grades have book boxes including text that is readable for them at 85 percent or higher fluency/word recognition, books within the genre they're working (if the unit is a genre study), thinking books (see Chapter 7), and other students' polished or published writing.

- During a genre study, students may be reading and writing in any genre, but spend most of the time focusing on the genre under study.

- These timelines are only suggestions. There are many ways to lay out the year in a Literacy Studio.

Intermediate Grades Literacy Studio Timeline

Unit	Timeline	Thinking Strategy	Reading/Writing Essential Standards
Launching the Literacy Studio	Last 2 weeks in August to 1st week in September	Integration of all seven strategies, often without naming them, to show how a proficient reader uses different strategies in a variety of ways	• Contrast narrative texts in written and spoken form. • Understand the process of collecting, planning, drafting, revising, and editing written pieces in several genres. • Understand the difference between polished and published forms of writing.
Narrative text including traditional literature	2nd week in September to 4th week in October	Monitoring for meaning; activating and creating schema; using sensory and emotional images	• Refer to details from the text when describing it. • Review narrative text elements. • Compare/contrast similar themes and topics in traditional literature. • Write narratives to develop real or imagined experiences.
Open genre	1st week in November to after Thanksgiving break	Continue monitoring for meaning, activating schema, and using sensory images	• Describe key differences in genres. • Compare/contrast points of view/narration.

Figure 3.5 Yearly Plan for Literacy Studio—Intermediate

continues

Intermediate Grades Literacy Studio Timeline

Unit	Timeline	Thinking Strategy	Reading/Writing Essential Standards
Informational Text	1st week in December to end of January	Asking questions; determining importance	• Cite details/evidence from text when describing it and/or inferring from it. • Decide which ideas are of greatest importance in a text. • Describe how authors use evidence to support claims. • Explain concepts and ideas accurately. • Compare and contrast primary sources with secondhand accounts. • Write informative/explanatory pieces including research to examine and build knowledge of a topic.
Open genre	1st week in February to Presidents' Day	Continue asking questions and determining importance; integrate other strategies that have been taught	• Identify and contrast themes and key ideas in several genres. • Recall relevant information from experiences to plan and organize a piece of writing in any genre.
Persuasive text	3rd week in February to 2–3 weeks prior to state testing	Inference and synthesis	• Refer to details when describing inferences about a text. • Write an opinion piece.
Persuasive text	Revisit informational text reading and writing 2–3 weeks prior to state testing	Revisit determining importance and synthesis	• Identify text structures (i.e., cause and effect, compare/contrast, chronological). • Interpret graphs, charts, tables, timelines, etc. and how graphic elements aid in comprehension. • Integrate information from two sources to write or speak effectively about a topic.

Figure 3.5 Yearly Plan for Literacy Studio—Intermediate, *continued*

Intermediate Grades Literacy Studio Timeline

Unit	Timeline	Thinking Strategy	Reading/Writing Essential Standards
Persuasive text	4 weeks following state testing	Integrate other strategies that have been taught	• Draw evidence from texts to support analysis or reflection.
Open genre	End of persuasive text unit to end of the year	Integration of all seven strategies, naming them to show how a proficient reader uses different strategies in a variety of ways	• Provide opportunities to read and write in a variety of genres; focus on students' intentions as readers and writers. • Provide differentiated supports on grade-level reading and writing standards.

Figure 3.5 Yearly Plan for Literacy Studio—Intermediate, *continued*

Primary Grades Literacy Studio Timeline

Unit	Timeline	Thinking Strategy	Reading/Writing Essential Standards
Launching the Literacy Studio	August through 1st 2 weeks of September (at most)	Thinking aloud to integrate all seven strategies, often without naming them to show how a proficient reader uses different strategies in a variety of ways	• Distinguish between narrative and informational text. • Use illustrations and graphics to describe key ideas. • Write stories in little books showing some use of text elements. • Respond to questions and suggestions from peers to revise stories.

Figure 3.6 Yearly Outline for Literacy Studio—Primary

continues

Primary Grades Literacy Studio Timeline

Unit	Timeline	Thinking Strategy	Reading/Writing Essential Standards
Informational text	2nd week in September—2nd week in October	Monitoring for meaning; schema for text content—text-to-self and text-to-world connections	• Identify key ideas and details. • Use text features such as tables of contents, headings, and glossaries to locate information. • Distinguish between information from graphics and information gleaned from the text. • Identify reasons an author uses to support points. • Identify similarities and differences between two texts on the same topic. • Write informational pieces with an introduction, information, and closure.
Genre choice	Last 2 weeks in October	Sensory and emotional images	• Begin to use digital tools to polish and publish pieces of writing. • Collaborate with peers to create writing in different genres.
Narrative text	1st week in November through December	Schema for text content and narrative text elements; text-to-self and text-to-text connections; asking questions	• Ask and answer questions about text. • Retell stories showing understanding of key ideas. • Understand narrative text elements: character, setting, conflict, sequence of events, resolution. • Identify who is telling the story. • Elaborate on a story using illustrations and details in the story. • Compare and contrast the experiences of characters in different stories. • Write narratives using narrative text elements, including temporal words to signal order; provide resolution.

Figure 3.6   Yearly Outline for Literacy Studio—Primary, *continued*

Primary Grades Literacy Studio Timeline

Unit	Timeline	Thinking Strategy	Reading/Writing Essential Standards
Genre choice	1st 2 weeks in January	Inferring across genres	• Describe the connection between two individuals, events, or ideas in narrative or informational text. • Write to show connections between individuals, etc.
Persuasive text	2nd 2 weeks in January	Determining importance	• Write opinion pieces with an introduction, an opinion, and closure.
Genre choice	February	Synthesis	• Participate in shared research and writing projects.
Informational text	March	Questioning	• Identify key ideas and details. • Use text features such as tables of contents, headings, and glossaries to locate information. • Distinguish between information from graphics and information gleaned from the text. • Identify reasons an author uses to support points. • Identify similarities and differences between two texts on the same topic. • Write informational pieces with an introduction, information, and closure.

Figure 3.6 Yearly Outline for Literacy Studio—Primary, *continued*

continues

Primary Grades Literacy Studio Timeline

Unit	Timeline	Thinking Strategy	Reading/Writing Essential Standards
Narrative text	April	Sensory and emotional images	• Ask and answer questions about text. • Retell stories showing understanding of key ideas. • Understand narrative text elements: character, setting, conflict, sequence of events, resolution. • Identify who is telling the story. • Elaborate on a story using illustrations and details in the story. • Compare and contrast the experiences of characters in different stories. • Write narratives using narrative text elements, including temporal words to signal order; provide resolution.
Genre choice	May	Integration of thinking strategies	• Participate in shared research and writing projects.

Figure 3.6   Yearly Outline for Literacy Studio—Primary, *continued*

I was lucky enough to be in the teachers' discussion I shared at the beginning of Chapter 2. I was quiet (quite a challenge for me). I listened to the teachers' very real concerns; I had heard these and others like them hundreds of times, and it struck me that there was a straightforward (notice I did not say easy) solution.

If we can cut our instruction time each day (by as much as half) by integrating reading and writing and if we can follow up by giving kids choice about how to experiment with their new learning, then we buy time for them to read and write independently, we buy time for us to confer with individuals and meet with small groups (configurations that are, by definition, more differentiated) who share a need or strength, and we may not feel defeated and overwhelmed as we take them to lunch.

We started to talk about this new conceptualization of workshop—the Literacy Studio—built around the idea that reading and writing are flip sides of the same coin and that so much of the content we teach should be learned through the reading *and* writing process. Really, why would we separate them? The teachers were intrigued and, as I hoped, peppered me with thoughtful questions, some philosophical, some related to "covering" the standards, some related to the logistics of the Literacy Studio, some related to how thinking strategy instruction might fit in, and all worth ongoing discussion. A couple teachers leapt in immediately and said, "I'm doing this tomorrow." Others were more inclined to consider it, read some of the descriptions I shared, and wait to hear how Literacy Studio went for the first teachers. All great!

The rest of this book is devoted to the opportunities you have to use time more effectively, address essential content, and have much more time to confer and hold small groups. We'll take the components one at a time. And, really, imagine walking your kids to lunch or releasing them into the packed hallways and thinking, "Wow, we got so much done this morning." Read on!

CHAPTER FOUR

All Together Now

Exploring the Craft of the Reader and Writer in Crafting Sessions

I t's early September in 2020, the year that will be etched in our collective consciousness. My life is profoundly changed, as yours has been. I am yet spared from the direct heartbreak so many others have experienced but the COVID-19 vaccine is a blip on the horizon, and I feel flashes of optimism. It is also one of the most challenging times in our civic life that I can remember. The summer of 2020 has been the setting for the ragged beginnings of long overdue conversations about systemic racism in this country. Certainly, there have been signs of progress in striving for racial equity over the preceding decades, but somehow the unrelenting quiet of the pandemic has given us time to come face-to-face with roiling injustices that have too long been repressed.

I have found that the quiet of holding still, solitary walks, and sleepless nights has exposed that unrest in many of us and the horror of the murders of George Floyd and far too many other people of color have amplified it. I find myself trying to listen more attentively, understand, and act—to acknowledge my privilege and work toward becoming an ally for people of color in this country. I hope that by the time this book is published our national attention to allyship will be much stronger. I know that when I get back to schools, my conversations with children will be different; I will not be afraid to tackle important issues, no matter how uncomfortable, with children gathered around me.

I am also acutely aware that teachers and students are among the great heroes of this pandemic, and they are exhausted. Others have articulated the profundity of our national admiration for educators far more eloquently than I'm able, but I know that teachers have approached this most trying of times with generosity of spirit, flexibility, and creativity beyond anything I could have imagined. And I know that for me, for educators around the world, children have been the reason we get up in the morning, the purpose we cling to, the joy we revel in, the animation of our lives. Simply, thank you to the nation's children and their teachers.

It has been a stationary time for me, and I do not hold still well. I walk with my eyes turned skyward, figuratively and literally. I miss being in the air; I miss my work. The thing I miss most is having kids gathered around me to read, write, and talk about words, books, art . . . Their ideas and insights, questions, and theories about the written word and the world never cease to engage and amaze me. I love the way they play off each other, lobbing ideas into the space, reacting, revising, imagining, testing theories, debating, questioning, gazing away lost in thought, working hard to understand. I could listen to them for hours. I have a very hard time bringing the conversation to a close and sending them back to work. I have a hard time saying no to a child who implores, "Just one more thing!" I revel in being in the company of children. (Joanne Hindley titled her book *In the Company of Children* and I've always thought it was the best title *ever.*)

I love those conversations, but children have also taught me to listen—no small feat. I had been the teacher who, uncomfortable with silence, blabbed away, sucking all the air out of the room, robbing the students around me of the gift of silence, the time to think. Not anymore. The times when I have students (of whatever age) around me to talk about language are air and water to my soul. I'm happiest then because I'm learning so intensely. As much as I enjoy being able to "see" kids through virtual visits, I need to see their eyes; I miss being able to sense when someone has something important to say, and I long for the time when I can walk around a classroom observing, taking notes, soaking it all in, just learning from them instead of frantically reading their comments in the chat box, trying to teach at the same time.

When I was an elementary student, we sat in desks, usually in rows, and waited our turn for our ten-minute small-group reading with the teacher. I remember trying to get teachers to notice me during those meetings, usually unsuccessfully. I adored my elementary teachers and desperately wanted to impress them; I usually didn't. We met in small groups, listened to the teacher, and walked away with worksheets to complete and were only allowed to read assigned excerpts of books out of the basal reader. "Free" reading was on Fridays at the end of the day. I ached for conversation, a teacher's reaction, kids to talk to who loved books as I did. So many teachers can relate; far too many students experience that worn-out routine today. The even sadder truth is that the students who need the stimulation of heterogenous group interaction the most get it the least. We're about to change all that. We're going to talk about inclusive whole-group instruction that looks, sounds, and feels robust and engaging to us and to children. We're going to spark discourse that makes it hard to say no when a student has "just one more thing" to say. We're going to talk about learning that introduces children to the scholar inside, that helps them build agency, that inspires them to experiment as readers and writers.

Perhaps most importantly, it is in part through our conversations with children about books and the issues in the world they describe that we ready them to take on the challenges of an inequitable world, a world in which their empathy, their sense of what is fair and just will, we hope, be a clarion call that is *heard* as perhaps no other generation has been heard. The foundation for these critically important life skills is here and now; there is no way to exaggerate its import. And we begin with children gathered around us.

I've never been comfortable with the term *minilesson*. The idea of "mini" teases the question, where is the real lesson? Is there a maxilesson? It feels, to me, like a prelude to the real thing.

Now, before the nation's teachers rise to decry my blasphemous assertion, let me clarify a couple of things. Whole-group minilessons (Crafting Sessions) should, generally, be short. We want to privilege the time students have to read and write over our tendency to pontificate (speaking only for myself, of course). Second, in this instruction we want to share one juicy strategy or tool for them to apply as readers and writers. We don't want to succumb to the feeling that, wow, they're actually paying attention, we've got them, they may even be engaged; maybe we can teach four concepts instead of the one we planned. How can we maximize the effectiveness of whole-group instruction, keep it reasonably brief, and still very engaging for children?

The Time Dilemma

So minilessons should be short. However. However, have you ever tried to read a book aloud (even a short picture book or essay) and think aloud to demonstrate the new reading strategy in ten minutes? Have you ever tried to model a new writer's craft move (Glover 2019) using your own writing while giving kids time to react and try it on their own in ten minutes? Can't be done. To shorten lessons, we've tried everything. We have tried district-mandated lesson durations; we have written dozens of pages of curriculum in a "perfect" sequence that we're supposed to teach during these minilessons; we've even cut back on the amount of text we share, opting to use excerpts of books or very short pieces in lessons. We've set timers, chastised ourselves for teaching too long. Still our lessons are, according to some, too long. But I've found that a great short text pulls kids in and doesn't let go. They don't want to stop in the middle with the promise of "more tomorrow." If we've chosen the book (or essay, or poem, or novel, or beautifully written informational text) thoughtfully, they lean forward to hear what's coming next. Our text choice is key to student engagement, and they're learning very important content about the social and natural world as we read aloud. And guess what? They want to *talk* about it. Right. Now.

Reading a complete text, a whole picture book, for example, lingering in it, discussing it and studying it carefully in one longer lesson not only capitalizes on the initial excitement about the text, but also helps kids internalize text elements (narrative) and text structure (informational). They need to hear the beginning, middle, and end—often in one sitting. They need time to think and talk to partners about it. They need to hear you think aloud about the lessons the text teaches both readers and writers. If you're modeling writing on a document camera, for example, they need to see where you're going with the piece, how you develop it; they need to see how the craft moves you're teaching work in a piece of writing. They need to see how you add, delete, and reorganize within your piece to make the meaning clearer. Ten minutes? Maybe, but I've noticed that too many writing lessons feel disjointed and that our promises of continuing tomorrow are often stymied because, well, school happens.

To complicate the time problem, we need to consider the efficiency (or lack thereof) of teaching a reading lesson *and* a writing lesson every day. That's twenty minutes with four transitions—coming and going from two lessons. Now, imagine that you want to integrate reading and writing into a single lesson as I discussed earlier. Ten minutes? Hmm, that's going to be tough. How realistic is the ten-minute minilesson?

> The structure of Literacy Studio allows for discovery, not only of the meaning of text, but equally important the craft of the author. Differentiation for multiple needs of students is more doable when we have the flexibility and large blocks of time focused on student practice and application. Teachers can ensure that students' needs are met by allowing students to grow in open-ended, goal-driven explorations of books and written expression. Critical and creative thinking is developed in conjunction with skill building, ensuring a balanced literacy approach for all.
>
> —Sascha Robinett, Principal, Milagro Elementary School, Los Angeles, CA

I believe that we need to think about time for whole-class instruction differently. Glance again at the planning wheel (Figure 4.1). If the portion from 12:00–8:00 represents the time students must read and write and the portion from 8:30–12:00 represents large-group instruction, our plan at least shows we're prioritizing students' independent work time (Composing). But let's think about the planning wheel as if it represented a *week* in the Literacy Studio.

If the ideal whole-class lesson length is ten to fifteen minutes, we have fifty to seventy-five minutes of whole-group (Crafting) time, *per week,* for reading *and* another roughly fifty minutes for writing, right? Let's revolutionize our use of time first by cutting that 100 minutes for instruction down to fifty to seventy, for *both* reading and writing. Then, let's divide that time in a way that best suits students and their level of engagement. If we have a thirty-minute Crafting Session that focuses on one learning intention as it applies to both reading and writing and we teach that on a Monday, for example, we have between twenty and forty-five minutes for whole-class instruction to divvy up

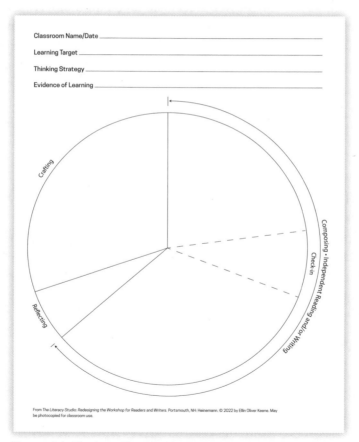

Figure 4.1 Thinking Flexibly About Your Schedule

across the remaining four days of the week. There may be a couple of days in which students come together for a two-minute reminder of class goals before launching directly into independent reading and writing (Composing). There may be three ten-minute lessons spread across the rest of the week. The permutations are endless. I believe that we get into trouble by looking at our instruction time *day by day* as opposed to *week by week*, or even in two-week segments. We can be far more flexible and still protect every minute of students' reading and writing time!

Look at a couple of sample elementary schedules based on a two-hour literacy block in Figure 4.2. The same schedules can be modified if you have ninety minutes or if your studio time is split into morning or afternoon, for example.

Sample 1

	Crafting (Minutes)	Composing (Minutes)	Reflecting (Minutes)
Monday	30	85	5
Tuesday	2	100	18
Wednesday	---	105	15
Thursday	20	90	10
Friday	10	100	10

Sample 2

	Crafting (Minutes)	Composing (Minutes)	Reflecting (Minutes)
Monday	5	100	15
Tuesday	30	80	10
Wednesday	---	110	10
Thursday	10	80	30
Friday	2	100	15

Figure 4.2 Sample Literacy Studio Schedules

Remember that in a Literacy Studio many, if not most, Crafting Sessions will incorporate reading *and* writing and Composing (more on this in Chapters 6 and 7) will encompass independent reading *and* writing. One lesson a day versus two. Two transitions instead of four. Crafting Sessions are meant to be very flexible, used as students need them, not an automatic, fixed-time, daily event whether they need it or not. Remember, the Literacy Studio plan is a *circle*! We can start anywhere, say Reflecting, and we can end anywhere. The schedule doesn't have to be lockstep, always beginning with a whole-group Crafting Session, followed by independent Composing time and concluding with Reflection. We might invite students to come into the classroom and begin Composing immediately, picking up where they left off the day before. In that scenario, the Crafting Session begins forty minutes into the Studio time.

Above all, the Literacy Studio is meant to be flexible enough that teachers can use the structure to best meet their students' needs. We need to free ourselves from rigid conceptualizations about how the time must flow and which groups we *must* see and, importantly, how long a Crafting Session has to be. Let's move on to what an integrated Crafting Session might look, sound, feel, smell (yep, keep reading), and taste (I hope not) like.

Before the Literacy Studio, students' responses were very surface level. They didn't fully understand what they were learning and why it was important. With the change I notice students applying what they have learned. Their reading and writing has improved. They add more details to their stories because they realize it is important based on skills we have practiced. For example, we just worked on sensory images and sensory details. Students realized that those details helped them as readers to create sensory images in their mind. A few of them went back to some stories they are working on and added more sensory details so their readers would know more about their story and their characters. Students were able to dig deeper into their reading and writing.

—Emily Lapp, fifth-grade teacher, Fire Prairie Upper Elementary, Fort Osage, MO

What, Exactly, Is a Crafting Session?

A Crafting Session includes everyone in the class and is focused on a learning target (such as a standard) that *everyone* needs and can apply as readers and writers. Crafting Sessions are held approximately two to four days per week for as short as five minutes or for as long as thirty minutes. Students interact with each other frequently through the lesson to work through the learning target and strategy you're sharing. They make decisions about what they're going to try as readers and writers based on your lesson once they get to Composing (independent work time for reading and writing).

Instead of holding one lesson focused on reading and another focused on writing, you can use any of the following formats for the Crafting Session:

- A lesson in which you remember to think aloud about how readers *and* writers can use the learning intention. For example, if you're focused on how readers generate questions about the text they read, you'll also remember to talk about how writers inspire their audience to wonder.

- A lesson in which you think aloud as you read and pivot to write and narrate your process to show how the learning target can be used in writing (or vice versa). For example, if your learning-target focus is nonfiction text structures, you might point out examples of cause and effect in a read-/think-aloud and then write to demonstrate cause and effect in your own writing.

- A lesson in which you think aloud as you read and pivot to write about the text you've just read. For example, if you're reading a persuasive piece aloud and focusing on inferring, you model how a writer infers when writing about that piece of text. In some districts, we call this written response to text.

- You may share students' writing or written responses to text in the Crafting Session so that students can see how their peers have begun to apply the learning target.

No matter how long or what your focus is, we're trying to create a particular tone in Crafting Sessions. At once scholarly and lively, serious and fun, engaged and anticipating ways they might try what you're teaching in reading and writing, students are all in! Thinking aloud and modeling (yes there is a difference—read the next section) are our primary teaching tools in a Crafting Session. To observe and react as a teacher reads or writes, pausing occasionally to share what they are thinking about—what and how they're planning as their next moves in reading or writing—is extraordinarily powerful. Children need that window into the mind of a proficient reader and writer as they work to apply the same concepts, strategies, and tools in their own work. As they think aloud, teachers often create a record of the new learning in the form of anchor charts or large class thinking notebooks; students use whiteboards and their own thinking notebooks to record responses and new learning they hope to apply as readers and writers. At the end of a Crafting Session, the teacher invites students to head off to try what they've learned as readers and writers. If they start by reading, they will switch to writing later in the Studio or the next day.

An In-Depth Look at a Crafting Session— What Does Literacy Studio Look Like, Day In and Day Out?

I was back at Tillman Elementary the following spring, and the fifth graders were gathered around me just after their lunch recess on a hot, sticky Florida afternoon. They were steamy, tired, and the odor was, well, eau de fifth grade, April edition. I had six teachers observing the lesson, and I was not feeling particularly optimistic about this one; the conditions were less than ideal. The fifth-grade team had asked me to focus on poetry. (It was April, after all—really, why do we only use poetry in April?) My job was just a small one, get kids motivated to write poetry in a ten-minute minilesson. I looked at the sea of faces before me and thought that maybe we should all be at the beach.

Some Background for the Lesson

The teachers on this team had, in the weeks leading up to this lesson, immersed students in poetry; encouraged students to choose and read poetry that interested them; urged them to linger with it, to reread and jot down what they noticed. The teachers used Crafting Sessions in the unit to think aloud about images, the thinking strategy they used to link all the concepts in the unit. They shared the images poetry evoked for them, discussed how poets use images to write poems, and took their cues for subsequent instruction from the images students shared and recorded. One teacher had composed poetry on the document camera spontaneously, another shared a poem she had written at home to get students to write poetry. Her students had dabbled with poetry in their writer's notebooks, but that wasn't going terribly well. I knew that they had read portions of Jacqueline Woodson's (2014) extraordinary memoir told through poetry, *Brown Girl Dreaming*, so I decided to use this text, in particular a short poem entitled "On Paper," to go deeper, perhaps even inspire some poetry writing.

The team had done a superb job building toward this lesson, but they had done it all with separate reading and writing lessons, reader's workshop,

writer's workshop. My job was to integrate reading and writing through the lens of sensory images. The teachers hoped to observe a Crafting Session that would meld reading and writing into a single lesson that could carry the kids into the next few days of their work. Their hope, like all of us, was to create more time for students to read and write independently. I also knew that a specific writer's tool might be helpful to give students something to experiment with in their writing. I chose to look at the use of white space in poems. As is true with virtually any concept we teach, learning targets such as using white

space connect to one or more thinking strategies. In a Literacy Studio, we are always thinking about how the disconnected skills and standards we are told to teach can become more integrated and relevant through the use of any of the thinking strategies. We ask, "What is the thinking my students need to do to apply this standard?" In this case, sensory images (see Thinking Strategies and Writer's Tools [available online, see page ix]) was our integrating strategy.

In planning with teachers over lunch prior to the lesson, I disavowed them of the notion that I was magically going to be able to get kids excited about writing poetry (especially not in ten minutes). The lesson would be longer; I predicted that it would take about thirty minutes. I also mentioned that we can't force engagement. If kids are going to be engaged, it must come from them (Keene 2018). Our goal was to build on all that they had already done, use poetry that draws kids in, think aloud about images that allow us to understand poetry more deeply, *and* invite them to think, as a writer would, about how poets do their work. We planned to ask them to collect words and images in their notebooks so we could share the experience of falling in love with the sound of words. A Crafting Session is the place to do all of that.

A Crafting Session

So there I was with twenty-five of my sweaty fifth-grade friends, thinking about how I could build on the beautiful work this team had already done.

I took a deep breath, waited for silence, and began without any words of explanation—I just read the poem "On Paper" (Woodson 2014). In the poem, Woodson writes of the joy she finds in simply writing her own name—she is an author, she can make her mark on the world. The poem is also a lovely evocation of a child's early realization that she can not only write her name but create marks on paper that *endure*. A writer can know the excitement of manipulating words into short phrases, longer stanzas, little clusters of meaning, and white spaces used purposefully. The poem evokes the moment she identifies as a writer and the transformation of words from her mind to words on a pure, unmarked sheet of paper. The writing is independent, her own foray into the world of a poet, a writer, unaided and personal.

How I hope our students experience those moments as they realize they are writers. My focus for the lesson was to offer the readers a *strategy* and the writers a *tool* they could use, not just today, but in the future when reading poetry and even prose and when writing. These tools would enable them to create images and manipulate space.

Setting the Tone—The Role of Silence and Teacher Language in the Crafting Session

After reading, I paused. I wanted the words to hang in the air for a moment or two. Some students looked around and squirmed. Why was this teacher just sitting there? Wasn't she going to make them do work?

In time, I greeted them, using the softest voice they could hear—I wanted the space to feel calm, but more importantly, I wanted to give the impression that we had the luxury of time, and we were about to have an experience that would impact them as readers and writers for a long time to come. I began:

Me: Good afternoon, ladies and gentlemen.

This was followed by a long pause. I began more slowly than most of us speak in whole-group lessons.

Instead of "Here's what we have to do today. I'm going to give you an example and then I want you to try it!" (I typed that really fast so that you would know to read those words at high velocity in your mind), I spoke, not slowly exactly, but as thoughtfully as I could, leaving lots of pauses to let my words sink in.

Me: I know you've been exploring poetry.

I paused, trying to visually connect with each student.

Me: I just shared a poem by Jacqueline Woodson from her book *Brown Girl Dreaming*. I'm going to reread it because poems are living things, and we need to hear them over and over to really understand and fully appreciate what the poet is trying to do.

I paused before rereading it. I could feel the tension from teachers and children—just get on with it. Why was she taking so long? Then, finally, there was a palpable sense of relief, an exhale, relaxing into the moment, tension draining, defenses being lowered.

Let me explain the silences, the pacing: In a Crafting Session, I value silence nearly as much as talk. Crafting Sessions aren't lessons in the way we typically think about lessons; they're all about *craft*. Crafting Sessions are the time to revel in words, to stand in awe of what an author has accomplished to make us feel a certain way; they're times for children to imagine how they might replicate these experiences another time, while working independently as readers and writers. Silence, time to think, matters a great deal in a Crafting Session. I don't want to break the spell, particularly in Crafting Sessions like the one I was conducting that day in Florida—the author's words do the work. I need to model what it is to be in awe of those words. I need to create the sense that magic happens here when we really listen to beautifully crafted text. The spell doesn't emerge from a high-speed, hastily worded cacophony of words spilling out of a teacher, with a couple of thirty-second opportunities to turn and talk where a child barely gets started and it's time to turn back around to face the teacher. The tone emanates from a great text, a sense of reverence for words, occasional repetition, rereading; the spell comes from realizing how lucky we are to be right here, right now, listening to just these words. It comes from trusting that less is more, that a great text will more than carry its weight in a lesson. It comes from strategically placed moments of silence.

Thinking Aloud

I reread "On Paper," without pausing. I wanted the words to settle inside the students and I wanted them to have the opportunity to experience the insights that nearly always come with a repeated reading. I didn't give background on the text, it's structure as a memoir in verse, or the author—the students were already exploring Woodson's book as a class. I don't always have the chance to read a piece in its entirety before thinking aloud, but with a very short piece, I try to capitalize on that opportunity.

And then it was time for instruction. Instruction is an *invitation* (not a lesson leading to an assignment) for students to think about the *craft* of the reader and writer, hence the term *Crafting Session*. It's an invitation to think about how they might consider and build upon how, in this case, Jacqueline Woodson, crafted the text, particularly how she used white space. Why did she, for example, position the word *becoming* on its own line? How did she use white space in this poem? What words and techniques did she use to cause us, as readers, to form images? What images might have inspired her as she wrote the poem? How did she connect this poem to the one before and the one after in her memoir of poems?

The Crafting Session is an opportunity for readers to discuss the *craft* of reading, how readers seek to understand more deeply. In this lesson, the learning target (which came from the teacher) was to think aloud about images and to be explicit about how images can help us understand. Using images is another tool readers and writers can learn to use to help them understand as readers and to make their writing more vivid.

Thinking aloud in a Crafting Session is one of the most powerful teaching tools we can use to give students insight into the ways we come to understand any text *and* how we consider ways to use writer's tools in our own writing. Thinking aloud is exactly (and no more) what it says it is. We pause while we write or read (in Crafting Sessions, conferences, or Invitational Groups) to say aloud what we're thinking at that moment, so that students can peer into the mind of a more skilled reader and writer, gaining insight into their thinking process and plans.

I want to be clear that I don't follow a sequence: first think aloud as a reader using images, then think aloud about how I might use single word lines and white space as a writer. I want to *weave* my thinking about reading and writing together, as seamlessly as I'm able. My ultimate goal is for students to become facile in thinking about reading and writing *simultaneously* and to be able to apply, as readers *and* writers, the craft moves we've talked about.

On the third reading of "On Paper," I paused to think aloud.

Me: Let me pause right here. I have an image in my mind; I wonder if it's what Jacqueline Woodson wanted me to see. I see young Jackie's hand curled awkwardly around a short pencil, with the eraser chewed off and teeth marks in the metal around where the eraser used to be. She has used this pencil until it's nearly a stub. I can almost hear the sound of the pencil on the paper. She is writing her name and the letters are big, misshapen, a little crooked. I wonder what Jackie Woodson did, as a writer, to help me form this image. But, you know what else I start to see? If I pause . . .

Which I did, to let the silence seep in around us and to give myself as well as the kids a chance to explore the image.

> **Me:** My image takes me further than just what I can see. As I visualize and hear the little hand writing her name, my image takes me beyond what I can see and hear into her mind and heart.

I paused again—time to think.

> **Me:** I can feel something that's just beginning in her, just the seed of a belief . . . but it's a belief that she has power. If she can write those words, she can write any words as she grows up, and that is power for a Black child who will have to confront racism and perhaps be ostracized by others. She is a girl, though, whose thoughts turn out to be strong and beautiful as she tells her life through these poems in *Brown Girl Dreaming*.
>
> I see her hand, I see the letters, but what I feel is power and because I know she went on to write so many books, I feel that as Jackie writes her name, she will find out that she can use her words to provoke new thinking in her readers and that she'll spark emotions, maybe enough to make her readers want to write. My image started with visualizing her hand, even hearing it move across the page, but it didn't stop there—my image turned into feeling that Jackie sensed the beginning of confidence inside her and, even if she wasn't aware of it as a little girl, she was starting to believe that she could change people's lives and the world through her writing.

I pointed out a line on the projected image of the poem that revealed Woodson's growing sense of independence. I didn't want to wait too long before pivoting to writing in the lesson.

> **Me:** I also want to think about how she used words and white space to help me think. I want to try to use white space in my own poems to convey something really important. See what I mean by white space? A poet uses the space throughout and around the poem to tell us important things about the meaning. You can do that in your own poetry!

I read through the word *becoming* all alone on its line before I paused for one more think-aloud.

Me: I want to think about this word, *becoming*. Jackie Woodson gives the word *becoming* its very own line in the poem. My image at this moment is of her words coming alive when others read them. I see all of us with her book in our hands, treasuring her published words and—wait a minute.

I paused for five or ten seconds—felt like a lifetime.

Me: In my mind that image of us holding her book is transparent; I can see through it. Below it, in my mind, I see my first image of her writing her name. It's the word *becoming* that helps me most. Becoming, like changing, transforming, evolving, emerging, blossoming . . . And I wonder, why did she give that word its own line, standing like a soldier, strong and alone and happy to be all by itself? What is important about that word becoming? Why, as a writer, would you give a word its own line? Look at all the white space around it!

I indicated the white space on the poem projected behind me.

Me: And you guys, why would she use only single spaces between some of these lines and double spaces after others? We just talked about how poets use white space to emphasize.

Hands shot up, but I looked down and away.

Me: Give me a second to think.

Silence. I read through the rest of the poem, slowly, softly, holding the words like gems and then paused. A bit more silence.

Me: I'm so curious to know what you're thinking.

Student Interaction

Gone was the sweaty fatigue of early afternoon. Nearly every hand went up, and some students popped up on their knees. The words had done their beautiful work. It was an obvious time to invite students to talk to a partner. I invited them to exchange ideas about two things pointed out on an anchor chart I had created before the lesson to help them remember their focus. It read: The *images* you had while hearing the poem and how, as a writer, Jackie Woodson used *white space* and her words to help you create images.

I've learned that the opportunities I've given for kids to talk during a Crafting Session are almost always too short. I walked around the group while they were sharing and inevitably, I noticed that the time to talk begins with a fair amount of shuffling, deciding who will go first (we can fix that one through instruction) and finally they get to the one, preplanned thing they wanted to share. Then, done!

Their initial sharing is rarely reflective of the depth and potential of their thinking. I've learned to listen in without engaging with pairs; I've learned to wait, listen, and push through the moment when they start to look to me to move on with the lesson. I often say,

> **Me:** Oh my gosh. Some of you are looking at me like you might have to stop sharing. Don't worry! You don't have to stop sharing after you've each said one thing. Ask each other, "What else?" and see what happens. Your partner will have so much more to say; you won't believe it!

Sometimes I restate what I've asked them to talk about, but after the awkward moment when they turn back to look at each other, the crescendo of talk begins and there is always, always more. We just need to be patient. In a Crafting Session, we create the conditions (see the online resources), the tone, that allows students to feel that they have all the time they need.

A final note: thinking aloud is not synonymous with modeling and demonstrating. See Chapter 5 for a description of important differences between these three teaching strategies.

The Send-Off

I sat back in front of the fifth graders and, very softly, said,

> **Me:** Would you please pivot your bodies so that you're facing me?

Just a quick word about my language use: I've been accused of using vocabulary that isn't common for children in the grade levels I'm teaching. I've been told it doesn't sound like kids' talk. So be it. I'm happy to live with that characterization because I'm going to take every opportunity in think-alouds to use vocabulary that *isn't* common for students. That's how vocabulary is learned. If we always use the words that kids use, how can we expect that they'll learn and use new words? I try to surround the use of a word like *provoked* and *transparent*, but also words like *becoming* (fifth graders may have some notion of what that word means), with other words to clarify and extend the meaning as in "Becoming, like changing, transforming, evolving, emerging, blossoming" earlier. I use *pivot* rather than "turn around and face me" because students will be engaging in the action that will make clear what *pivot* means. See the Talk About Understanding principles in Chapter 2 or *Talk About Understanding* (Keene 2012) for much more on the use of sophisticated vocabulary and syntax in Crafting Sessions.

Once the students were back, I took a few moments to hear about their conversations.

Me: So, I'd love to hear about your conversations with partners.

Hands shot up throughout the room.

Me: I'm curious . . .

Long pause.

Me: To hear if your *partner* had insights about our two questions. How do images help you understand more deeply in this poem and in anything you're reading? And how does a poet provoke images in readers, especially through the use of white space in a poem?

Not so many hands. Kids leaned toward partners, trying to be surreptitious, asking to be reminded of what the partner said. Next time, I thought, they'll be listening just a bit more closely.

Winter raised her hand to share what her partner, Rochelle, had said.

Winter: Rochelle said that she [the poet] used white space to make you slow down and think about it.

Jovani followed immediately.

Jovani: Yeah, we said that too. We said you can get images if you stop at the white space. It's like a stop sign.

Me: I'm so interested in those insights. Would you mind adding them to the anchor chart we've started? But first I want to ask you something, Winter and Rochelle. Did you talk about how you could try to use white spaces in your own poems to make the reader slow down and think about it?

Rochelle: Nope, but you could.

Me: Oh my gosh, you two! Are you going to try that as poets today?

They nodded immediately. I'm quite sure that it had never entered their minds! I knew before the lesson that Winter was one of the children who was not writing poetry.

Me: OK, here's the deal. Go up and add your ideas about using white space on the anchor charts and then go! I don't want you to waste another minute. Get started on your poems and use white space to help your readers slow down to create images as they read.

They looked perplexed—wait, you want us to go write while everybody else is here? I nodded and gestured for them to get going. They created a bit of a stir getting the markers and deciding what to write on the anchor chart. Several other students reminded them of what they had said, and they got to work. Note to self: remind kids to write in big enough letters on anchor charts that I don't have to use a magnifying glass to read the words. Then, off they went. Both got out their writer's notebooks and dug in. I didn't know what they were writing, but at least they were writing. Maybe Winter was using *nothing but* white space in her poem, but she appeared to be writing something.

I love to send kids off with a sense of urgency and in a staggered fashion to work even before the official Crafting Session is over. They serve as models for what other students will soon do, and the message "Don't waste a moment; you have so much to say!" is one I want very much to communicate to the whole class.

I invited two other partnerships to share—both focused on images they had when I read the poem and were eager to add their images to the anchor chart. The images were a great start. Ultimately, I want everyone to walk away with new strategies they can use, not just for *this* poem, or *today's* work, but reaching far into the future—that's the definition of a strategy. I want them as high school students and adults reading to their own children to think about images, the poet's use of white space, and the connection between the two. Crafting Sessions aren't just for today. Strategies aren't just for today.

The topics we address in Crafting Sessions are *worthy* of children's ongoing attention and use. If the topics I address in Crafting Sessions aren't important enough to be applied for the rest of their lives as readers and writers, I need to rethink that lesson. Crafting Sessions are meant to inspire readers and writers. They're meant to raise the stakes, push their thinking, make their work just a bit more challenging and therefore, qualitatively better.

I needed to make this staying power clear to the students.

> **Me:** OK, you guys shared some really amazing images that you conjured as you heard this poem, but here's what's very important to me. I want to know how images help you as readers and writers, not just today or in this poem, but how using images will help you change as a reader.

I know that's a question that must be asked repeatedly. They need to learn to expect that question: How will (the strategy) _____ help you as a reader and a writer in other situations including those outside of school?

They looked at me. I looked at them. I smiled. They continued to look at me. I smiled. They started to regard me as if I had landed recently from another planet. There was silence—not the good kind. Or maybe it was because Silvia piped up.

> **Silvia:** Well, why can't we make images if we're reading long books?
>
> **Me:** Like novels, Silvia?
>
> **Silvia:** Yeah, like why do you only have to do it in your mind in poems?
>
> **Me:** Well, exactly, Silvia. So, what should we remember, for a long, long time about using images? What would you tell other readers or writers about using images?

Jovani, the original image maker was back in the game.

> **Jovani:** Oh, like you could tell them that whatever you're reading, you can slow down and make pictures in your mind.
>
> **Me:** So interesting, Jovani. You're going to write that on the anchor chart?

He nodded.

> **Me:** So, you're talking about making pictures in your mind. That's a big part of it. Remember, though, when I had a picture in my mind that led to a . . .

I paused.

Several students (blurting out simultaneously): A feeling!

Jovani: Oh yeah, OK, so you can slow down and see something in your mind, and it can make you feel something?

Me: I think so. I think an image can lead you to understand almost anything in any book, if you take the time to focus on it in your mind and in your heart. I think images help readers understand and I think writers of all kinds of books may be inspired by images and they may work to use words (and white spaces if they're poets) to provoke images in their readers.

Jovani headed to the anchor chart and wrote, in slightly larger letters, "Stop, slow down, let images make you see and feel things about the book." Not bad, gang, not bad!

It was time to transition to the Composing Session, one of the most critical moments in the Crafting Session. It is here that I want to invite students to apply what we've discussed. I must be so careful here, so precise.

I lowered my voice; they leaned in.

Me: Today, ladies and gentlemen, we've talked about so much just from this one powerful poem. We've talked about strategies, like creating images, you can use not just today, but throughout your lives as readers and writers. We talked about how images can deepen your understanding of a book and how writers strive to help their readers create images as they read. We've also talked about how poets are inspired by images and how they write using images and how they use white space in a poem to help readers stop, think, create images, wonder, reread. Poets use white space to emphasize one idea.

Now, who's ready to try it? You have a choice today. Some of you will go to Composing to try out what you've learned as you read poetry (or other things you're reading) and some of you will choose to write poetry, thinking about images that can become poems and remembering to use white space strategically while you're trying to provoke images in your readers. Now, I'd like to know now who will work first today as a reader.

There followed considerable conversation and confusion—was I really sure that they could choose whether to read or write? I was. How did they know which to do?

Me: OK, if you think about all we've learned, you'll know that you want to start trying to use images and pay attention to white space in poetry as either readers or writers. You'll do both; just think about where you'll start.

About two-thirds of the children indicated that they would read. I was a little disappointed that it wasn't closer to half, but I had about eight writers including the two who had already started.

Me: Great. If you're going to work as a reader, you may go now, settle in with whatever you're reading and be on the lookout for the poet's use of white space. Think about why they used this white space and pay attention to your images. How do your images help you understand that poem better? How does the poet's use of white space allow you to pause, reflect, and even come up with an image or two? What images might have inspired the poet or writer you're reading? Use your thinking notebooks to record anything that you think you've really learned as a reader today. We'll talk about that in Reflecting time.

We paused as the readers went off to their work and I narrated their progress a bit.

Me: Look at them, you guys.

I said to the remaining kids who intended to write. Then, loudly enough to be heard by the whole class:

Me: Great! As the readers are finding their spots, you're going to see them getting comfortable with their books. Some are poetry books, I see. Others are reading different types of books, but everyone is going to be thinking about images, how they help us understand more deeply and how writers use them to lead us to deeper understanding. It will be interesting to see if they keep reading for the rest of the Literacy Studio or if they shift to writing poetry at some point during Composing. If they switch, they'll have to make a note of that in their thinking notebooks. Now, are you ready to write? What do you need?

Student: Can I start a new poem? I don't like the one I have.

Me: What do you think I'm going to say to that?

Student: Yes?

I just smiled and nodded. I used a silent signal, one hand mimicking writing on the palm of the other, and needed to say no more. They were off, these writers.

The room had that great buzz we all cherish. I always reserve the first few minutes to move around the room, taking notes on student engagement. Some were reading with intent. Some were writing with intent. Some took time to get focused. A couple never got engaged. But those who did read and write were focused on the same concepts: a strategy (creating sensory and emotional images) that will be useful for both readers and writers (see Figure 4.3 for reading and writing ideas and the online resources for all thinking strategies and their direct ties to writing) and a tool (a writer's use of white space) they can experiment with as readers and apply as writers. (The Thinking Strategies online resource also includes a number of writer's tools that may be helpful for writing instruction that connects to reading.) I didn't need two "mini" lessons. The whole thing was over in about twenty-five minutes, and the kids were off to the most important part of the day—reading and writing, the Composing time (stay tuned for that in Chapter 6). Chapter 5 will take us into the nitty-gritty of Crafting Sessions and help us make the transition to Composing.

In the time at home, I've been forced to develop a skill I have always sorely lacked—patience; also, tech skills I never wanted, teaching via Zoom and Meets, and thinking about how to promote student (and teacher) engagement through a screen. I hope I can carry the patience into postpandemic life. I hope the lessons of empathy, trust, innovation, simplifying without dumbing down, rule-breaking, risk-taking, and improvisation will serve me and the teachers and students with whom I work in the coming years. There must be something to cherish from this time, and it certainly isn't those peaceful moments with clouds at my feet.

In simplicity we find the greatest elegance. So, for now, here's what I know. Diverse text matters. Integration matters. Choice matters. Talk matters. I wonder if this should be a nine-word book. Nah . . .

Figure 4.3 shows the list of key ideas related to sensory and emotional images from which I drew to create the images portion of the lesson. In the online resources, you'll find a similar list for each comprehension strategy and its connection to writing.

Sensory and Emotional Images

Readers

▶ Readers create sensory images during and after reading. These images may include visual, auditory, and other sensory as well as emotional connections to the text and are rooted in prior knowledge.

▶ Readers use images to draw conclusions and to create unique interpretations of the text. Images from reading frequently become part of the reader's writing. Images from a reader's personal experience frequently become part of their comprehension.

▶ Readers use their images to clarify and enhance comprehension.

▶ Readers use images to immerse themselves in rich detail as they read. The detail gives depth and dimension to the reading, engaging the reader more deeply, making the text more memorable.

▶ Readers adapt their images in response to the shared images of other readers.

Figure 4.3 Sensory and Emotional Images

continues

> ▶ Readers adapt their images as they continue to read. Images are revised to incorporate new information revealed through the text and new interpretations as they are developed by the reader.

Writers

> ▶ Writers consciously attempt to create strong images in their compositions using strategically placed detail. They include just enough detail to spark images in their readers.

> ▶ Writers create impact using strong nouns and verbs whenever possible.

> ▶ Writers use images to explore their own ideas. They consciously study their mental images for direction in their pieces.

Figure 4.3 Sensory and Emotional Images, *continued*

CHAPTER FIVE

From Crafting to Composing

How It All Comes Together

Now that you have been introduced to the integration that goes into a Crafting Session, it's time to talk about the good stuff. Down to the bones—*what* do we integrate and *how* do we do it? If you buy in (at least for the moment) to the idea that we need to integrate reading and writing content to engage kids, give them more choice, and allow us to deepen instruction, we've got to talk about the tools we use to do that in the Crafting Session. First, let's take a bit closer look at Crafting Sessions. We'll start with a quick list of the elements we weave together in a Crafting Session and work our way into some helpful tools for Crafting Sessions in your classroom.

A Closer Look at Crafting Sessions

SOME KEY IDEAS FOR CRAFTING SESSIONS
(WHOLE-CLASS LESSONS IN READING AND WRITING)

- **Teacher think-alouds** help children peer into the mind of a proficient reader or writer—most frequently, reading and writing are taught in the same lesson. Pause for a think-aloud at key turning points in fiction and big ideas in nonfiction, but be careful not to interrupt the flow of the text too much. Three think-alouds while reading a picture book are usually enough. I'll go into much more depth on think-alouds later in this chapter.

- The **literature or informational text** a teacher chooses is fundamental to the success of the lesson—select text that is beautifully written, represents diverse authors and content, has layers of depth and room for interpretation, and is conducive to thinking aloud for reading and select authors whose craft you can scrutinize for writing. As a rule, select read-aloud text that will challenge students' thinking. Children may be reading and writing at a wide variety of "levels," but they can all think deeply!

- **Clarity** about the teaching intention leads to precise and elegant language in the lesson—precise and elegant language leads to a tone of rigor, inquiry, and intimacy. Don't be afraid to use vocabulary that is more developed than the children's spoken vocabulary. That's how they acquire and learn to use new words!

- **Modeling** from your own experience grounds the lesson in the real world—read and write as the children observe, and talk about your life as a literate person. Modeling helps students develop and refine an identity as readers and writers.

- Help children see **connections** beyond today—how they can use this learning target in other contexts, including in the content areas. Crafting Sessions focus on helping children become independent readers and writers who solve problems independently with tools you've modeled.

- Use **silence** to help children understand the gravity of certain points and to reinforce that readers and writers take their time to think before responding and that the teacher won't simply move on to the next child with their hand raised. The best thinking often takes the longest time. Don't give up after one exploratory response. Invite them to deepen their original thinking. My favorite two words in a Crafting Session? "What else?"

- Limit the **focus** of the lesson to one teaching intention (e.g., how readers and writers use questions to create meaning) unless the goal is to link to previously learned material. This is hard, isn't it? Try to use the Crafting Session as a way to connect what they have learned, but stay focused as much as possible!

- Send them off to **meaningful** independent work in the Composing Session. This is their chance to try what you've shown them in the Crafting Sessions.

A note about word learning in a Crafting Session: Most word learning, including phonics and word analysis is best taught at the moment a child needs it, in reading aloud or writing through conferences and needs-based small groups like Invitational Groups. Therefore, word learning is rarely taught to the whole class in a Crafting Session unless the teacher is certain that all students need that skill.

WHEN YOU DO FOCUS ON WORD LEARNING IN THE WHOLE GROUP, PLEASE KEEP THE FOLLOWING IN MIND:

- Crafting Sessions focused on word learning should be **short**, **engaging** lessons including phonics practice, word play, categorizing words, rhyme, song, and games and generally for primary-aged children.

- **Focus** on learning targets truly needed by the *whole class*; we must avoid teaching word skills to students who are already applying those skills in their reading and writing.

- **Record and post** children's learning around the classroom for later reference—encourage children to use posted records when **solving problems** at the word and sentence level as readers and writers.

- Help children see **connections** beyond using the strategy or tool today or in this book and how they can use these tactics independently each time they read and write.

- **Demonstrate** use of the skill in text and writing so children can see real-world applications.

- Following any Crafting Session (and sometimes before—remember the alternative schedules from Chapter 4), we send them off to **meaningful independent work** in a Composing Session.

Brushes, Paints, and Canvases: Your Tools for Crafting

Now you have an idea about what Crafting Sessions are all about. Imagine for a moment that you're a painter working in a studio with canvases and brushes and paint of every color at your fingertips. You have an image in your mind that you want to capture. Your hands move over paints and brushes until you have collected the perfect combination—this brush, starting with that color on this type of canvas. You'll revise and paint over what you start, probably many times, until the image emerges from the canvas and comes to life. But it starts with collecting the right tools. Never ever (except perhaps in school) is a painter told which brush, which canvas, which colors to use—they would laugh at the idea. The image is theirs; they will choose the combination of tools to realize it.

Your Literacy Studio is exactly the same. You have a palette of tools from which to choose to bring forth the image—students' learning—you

wish to create. You make those choices carefully based on your knowledge of curriculum, instruction, feedback options, and most importantly, what your students need and are striving to work on. Never ever should you be told exactly how to wield those tools; you know your students, you know what you imagine and hope for them, you understand their needs and desires as readers and writers, and now you'll have a repertoire of tools from which to choose.

The remainder of this chapter is designed to equip your studio for Crafting and beyond. You'll make the choices about which curriculum and instructional tools to use based on your intimate knowledge of your students and their needs. I've collected the brushes and paints that I share below after years and years of experimentation; I've never ever used the same tools in the same way twice. We'll talk in this section about three sets of tools from which you can pick and choose for use in your Crafting Sessions. You know many of these already, and there are an infinite number of variations in how you can use them.

HERE ARE YOUR BRUSHES!

1. Instruction moves

   ◆ Thinking aloud

   ◆ Modeling

   ◆ Demonstrations

HERE ARE YOUR PAINT COLORS!

2. The learning targets in literacy: concepts, tools, and strategies (defined in Chapter 4 but can also include standards, processes, craft moves, curriculum, and areas of focus that will never find their way into a standards document—think developing characters or manipulating white space in poetry!)

   ◆ Writer's tools

   ◆ Strategies for readers and writers (see the online resources)

HERE ARE YOUR CANVASES!

3. Materials

   ◆ Wide range of text complexity in your library

   ◆ Very diverse texts—written as windows, mirrors, and sliding doors for your readers (Bishop 1990)

Let's start with instruction moves. There are thousands of teaching tactics, including gimmicks out there. You've tried a lot; many have worked, some not so much. Let's focus on the three instructional moves we know to be most effective in literacy instruction. You can apply every ounce of your teaching artistry to finding variations on these three themes.

Part 1: The Brushes: Instruction Moves for Crafting Sessions That Integrate Reading and Writing

Thinking Aloud

SHOWING HOW READERS AND WRITERS *THINK*

- Teachers read aloud or write publicly, pausing to explicitly narrate their thinking processes (see think-aloud example in Figure 5.1).

- Teachers are clear about how the learning target (concept, strategy, tool, standard) on which they're focused helps them read or write more fluently, comprehend more deeply, or write more effectively than they would without it.

- Teachers work to ensure precision in their think-alouds, focusing on the most universal application of the concept—how can readers and writers expect to use this target going forward?

- Teachers resist the urge to think aloud about the most obvious content or new vocabulary in the text or to focus on what can be observed directly in writing, opting instead for the kind of deep thinking and meaningful writing they hope to see in students' work.

- Teachers are clear in describing how students can apply the concept independently.

Sample Think-Aloud Focused on Reading and Writing

Read through the sample think-aloud in Figure 5.1. In developing this lesson for a third-grade class, I intended to integrate reading and writing into a single lesson that focused on Inferring (the strategy/learning target) for readers and writers. I wanted to open doors for students to experiment with inferring about the internal lives of book characters and to try to develop the internal lives of characters about whom they're writing. In this case, the Crafting Session included the book *The Three Questions* by Jon Muth. *The Three Questions* is a lovely allegory based on a children's adaptation of the Tolstoy story of the same name, in which three animals struggle to find the answers to three questions: When is the best time to do things? Who is the most important

Integrated Think-Aloud That Includes Reading and Writing

After reading to page 2

When I first start to read about Nikolai, I realize that he has certain qualities that I wish I had. When I read about how serious and pensive he is, how focused on trying to understand the most important questions in life at such an early age, I realize that there is something that we might all learn from as we try to understand the world. I want to work on characters like Nikolai. I want to show what my characters are like on the inside. I want my readers to be able to infer to understand what they think, feel, and believe. Right now, I'm worried that I write about the same types of characters over and over. Tomorrow, when I'm writing "aloud," I hope you'll help me try out a different kind of character in my work.

After reading to page 7

These pages really make me think about the writing I'm doing now. I am going to jot down some things that I know my characters think, feel, and believe rather than just what they do. I want my characters to know who they are—what they believe, what makes them want to act. Here's what made me think about that: When I read about Nikolai's friends' hasty responses to his important questions, as a reader I inferred that, even though we have good friends we trust, sometimes the answers to the most important questions come from ourselves. I want to try a character in my writing who thinks a lot about questions in their life. In *The Three Questions*, I infer that Nikolai is dissatisfied with the other characters' responses because he knows that the answers to questions as important as these should come from himself and his experiences.

After reading to page 17, after the panda and her baby are reunited in Leo's home

I'm predicting that because Nikolai played such an important role in the rescue of the panda and her baby, he will begin to realize that his questions may be unanswerable or that, if there are answers, they will have to come from him thinking about his own actions and how those actions helped him to understand *When is the best time to do things? Who is the most important one?* and *What is the right thing to do?* I'm so interested in unanswerable questions. Do you think that, as a writer, I can build in some questions that my character thinks about, but can't really answer? How would that work?

   As a reader I also infer, though our questions may be different from Nikolai's, that this author is trying to tell us that it is very important that we have big questions about how the world works and that it is one of our jobs in life to consider the elusive answers to those questions. I think that when we ask those questions and seek the answers, we may be more able to help others, just in the way that Nikolai did.

Figure 5.1 Integrated Think-Aloud That Includes Reading and Writing

one? What is the right thing to do? In one character's moment of crisis, the answers are revealed.

Note: In the next day's lesson the teacher wrote in front of the students (a write-aloud), to show how to create opportunities for a writer's audience to infer. The teacher referred to the inferences from the previous day's lesson to talk about how writers leave out just enough information or detail to allow their readers to infer. In both lessons, the teacher can show how to develop the character's internal life—what they think, feel, and believe.

In this think-aloud, I tried to focus on thinking aloud about inferences in a clear, precise way without overdoing the think-aloud to the detriment of the story. I worked to integrate writing knowing that the teacher would focus more on writing the next day. The important concept to keep in mind was that I was very explicit in thinking aloud. For example, "Here's why I'm thinking that." And in the think-aloud following page 17, instead of focusing only on predicting, a type of inference, I talked specifically about *why* I predicted and wove reading and writing into the think-aloud. I moved from the focal (the text itself) to the global (issues beyond the book and classroom) in the final section. This anchors the think-aloud in a broader context, the role of pondering unanswerable questions, and places a clear value on the importance of pondering those questions.

Thinking aloud is a powerful instructional tool—it's worth practicing; I feel as though I've been working to perfect it every year of my life in education. There is no *wrong* idea to think about, no *wrong* way to think aloud—it's fun to watch how practice makes our think-alouds better. Thinking aloud allows students to observe the mind work of another reader and writer and to practice new ways of approaching the text they read and compose.

Now, during our Literacy Studio time, we let our reading inform our writing and our writing goals inform our reading. We engage in inquiries, reflect, study, grow, and discuss our process and craft. In doing so, our instructional time is more collaborative and student driven. There's more of everything! More books and students' writing to read, create, collect, share, learn from, and be inspired by.

—Modesta Urbina, third-grade teacher, Milagro Elementary School, Los Angeles, CA

Modeling

SHOWING HOW READERS AND WRITERS *BEHAVE*, WHAT THEY DO TO LIVE AN ENGAGED LITERATE LIFE

- Teachers describe their lives as readers and writers—where and when they like to read; how they choose books; what they prefer in relation to author's style, content, and genre; how they choose writing topics and plan their writing; and what tools and craft moves they like to use (see examples at the end of this chapter).

- Teachers help students develop and describe their own preferences as readers and writers including what authors they love and which topics resonate most for them as writers.

- Teachers help children develop an identity as a reader and writer through discussion, catching them in the act of trying new strategies and tools and naming what they try.

- Teachers create a classroom environment conducive to in-depth learning—there are spaces conducive to group work, independent work, and small-group discussion; books, texts, and writing materials are accessible; and records of children's thinking, class goals, and group ideas line the walls. Students' identities and strengths are highlighted through photographs of them at work.

- Teachers ensure that learning experiences are authentic—that what they ask students to do in class is something readers and writers might choose to do outside of school.

Let's think about the first few weeks of school. You want to get to know the students and you want them to know you. This is a perfect time to talk to them about your identity as a reader and writer—what books you treasure from your past, what written pieces you're most proud of, what you struggle with as a reader and writer, your preferences, and importantly, how you use books to help you write and revise and how your reading affects your writing and vice versa.

I always tell kids that I'm happiest as a reader and writer with a couple of basset hounds in the room! Their sweet breathing (OK, snoring and drooling!)

helps me concentrate, and they provide a lovely break when I get too tied to the computer. When modeling, we're cognizant of the ways we hope our student readers and writers will learn to live in the literate world. We can certainly overmodel, so it's worth being aware that we only share our lives as readers and writers as a way to invite them to develop and share themselves.

Demonstration

HOW DO READERS AND WRITERS INTERACT WITH EACH OTHER IN THE LITERACY STUDIO?

- Teachers demonstrate or assist in student demonstrations designed to show the rituals and routines that lead to and sustain community in the classroom throughout the year (see the rituals and routines section under "Part 2: The Paints" [page 93]).

- Teachers set up walk-through demonstrations in which students enact the processes of obtaining resources and materials (i.e., book and writing topic selection) in the classroom or transition from one activity to another.

- Teachers demonstrate or assist in student demonstrations to show how students share their thinking about books via oral, written, artistic, or dramatic means (how book clubs, think-pair-share, turn-and-talk, and other interactions work).

- Teachers demonstrate the process of peer conferring in response to a text and in response to another writer's piece—how to listen actively and give helpful feedback through questioning.

- Teachers show through "fishbowl" types of demonstrations how students can build on other students' ideas in discussion and how they can use "open forum" in which the whole group converses about a book or another student's writing.

I confess that classroom management is always on my mind. I worry about what other kids are up to when I'm conferring with one; I'm bothered by unnecessary movement around the classroom; I'm easily distracted by voices that are too loud. I wish I could tell you that I'm more Zen. I need to know that the classroom is well organized and that students take a great deal of responsibility for their own movement and interaction with other students.

If I have to intervene more than once on a particular issue, for example, that's a signal that I need to build in a demonstration, a walk-through focused on a sticky part of the Studio. If kids have a difficult time getting focused on reading and writing at the beginning of Composing, we need to re-create that time so that we can all demonstrate for each other what a smooth transition from Crafting to Composing looks like. If it doesn't work the next day, it's back to practice in another demonstration. Sometimes it takes two or three demonstrations or a repeated demonstration later in the year to get these rituals and routines down. We're giving kids time, choice, and autonomy in Literacy Studio, which pays off in their level of engagement, but it may mean more investment in demonstrations throughout the year to create the conditions conducive to focused reading and writing.

So for me, demonstrations are the key to managing a Literacy Studio. Please see pages 97–100 for a list of demonstration lessons that can be used throughout the year to maximize efficiency and minimize disruptions in the Literacy Studio.

Thinking aloud, modeling, and demonstrating are three powerful instructional tools, the brushes you use to achieve just the right impact in the Studio. You can pick and choose among them to provide variety in your instruction and to ensure that your students perceive you as another reader and writer who struggles and succeeds, sets new goals, and works to understand more deeply and write more clearly and movingly.

Part 2: The Paints: Concepts, Strategies, and Tools for Crafting Sessions

We are teaching in a standards- and assessment-driven world. I understand the need to address agreed-upon state standards, but too often students aren't driven to learn what can be very dry concepts. How many years can we ask students to cite evidence and supporting details to back up a claim about what the author (we assume) thought the theme or main idea was? By contrast, children sit up and take notice when we, for example, show that some conflict is external to the characters in fiction and some conflict is internal. This feels like the real stuff that writers use. I've yet to see internal and external conflict in an elementary state standards document, but I teach it all the time to children as young as second grade. Why not? It improves their writing, takes their comprehension to another level, and is engaging. I'm not suggesting that we forgo teaching the concepts from our standards document, but we can supplement some of the same old, tedious concepts we teach every year with concepts that intrigue and engage. Therefore, in this section, I'll focus mostly on learning targets, tools and strategies *that you aren't likely to find in your state standards* but that are important for your readers and writers nonetheless. I share these in the form of lists that are meant to be used as resources to complement your district's curriculum. Others have written eloquently about how and when to teach this content (Fletcher and Portalupi 2006; Glover 2019) and detailed descriptions of each strategy and tool aren't within the scope of this book, but you will find that these strategies and tools provide depth and dimension to your teaching making it much more likely that students will retain and reapply what they have learned.

Strategies and tools comprise, along with standards and curriculum, the learning targets, the *concepts* or content in reading and writing instruction.

You'll remember that for our use, *tools* are the techniques a reader or writer uses in a specific text or genre, like exploring character change in fiction, and *strategies* are the thinking moves readers and writers use that will be applicable in nearly every context or genre, like using sensory images. These paint colors, along with your state's standards, are the *content*, the *what* of literacy instruction in the Literacy Studio, and can usually be taught in reading and writing simultaneously.

The strategies and tools I've chosen to share here may seem ambitious—a good thing, right? Some would doubt that elementary-aged students are able to understand and embrace these concepts. My experience has been just the opposite. Students love to learn concepts that help them feel like the real readers and writers they are! Using teaching tactics like thinking aloud, teachers can be precise about their use of these tools in texts (and your writing) that are appropriate for the students with whom you work. I prefer to trust the children to embrace and choose the tools and strategies that work for them. I'm rarely disappointed.

Here are the paint colors . . . experiment away!

Learning Targets: Strategies and Tools for Readers and Writers

Strategies are the tactics readers use to understand text more deeply and also some techniques writers use to manipulate (in the best way) their readers as they create meaning in writing. Strategies are taught because they will serve readers and writers in nearly any text and in every genre they read and in many writing contexts. Strategies aren't just "the skill" you master today; they have staying power in many, many reading and writing contexts. Strategies include, for example, thinking strategies such as using schema, questioning, synthesizing, inferring, and so on. (See Thinking Strategies and Writer's Tools [available online, see page ix].)

Tools are the techniques writers use to make their reading and writing more potent in particular kinds of writing, within a genre, for example. Using dialogue in narrative text or using text features in informational text to understand more clearly are examples of tools. Tools may not be useful in everything students read and write, but they will help students think like a writer and write beautifully for a particular audience. (Thinking Strategies and Writer's Tools includes a full list of writer's tools.)

As you consider which strategies and tools to use, remember that there isn't a right strategy or tool to use at any given time. It really is more about the process of choosing what to teach based on observed student needs. Think about these questions:

- What kinds of reading and writing are students attempting (either because they chose to do so or because you're engaged in a genre study)?

- What are the key features of the genre?

- What challenges might students face in the genre in which they are reading and writing?

- What appealing texts might you use as mentors for this unit?

Let's take a closer look. Let's imagine that you want to help first graders take on their first research project, a topic that appears in the Common Core State Standards (National Governors Association Center for Best Practices, Council of Chief State School Officers 2010) in grade 1. (For an intermediate-grade version of this lesson, see page 138.) Alongside the standard (participate in shared research and writing projects), you might want to focus on a strategy and a tool or two. For example, asking questions (see Thinking Strategies and Writer's Tools online) might be a strategy to use to lead into topics about which young children are curious. Perhaps they could keep track of questions and topics they wonder about for a couple of weeks, leading into the shared research project. You could think aloud to share your questions as you read informational texts while encouraging the children to keep track of their own questions.

As you get closer to the time when you undertake research, you might introduce several tools writers use to make their informational writing more compelling. You will want the children to consider the purpose and an audience for their research: Why is it important to share what they learned? How will it make a difference to their audience? You might want to reread several informational texts kids enjoyed in studying the way authors use interesting leads and endings to engage their audience. Finally, let's help children see how repetition or the length of time spent explaining an idea in informational text can be used to underscore its importance.

No matter what grade you teach or what standards you must address, supplementing instruction with strategies and tools will help students practice more authentic and engaging language use and retain and reapply what they have learned. Use Thinking Strategies and Writer's Tools to pick and choose strategies and tools that align with your goals and your students' interests.

Demonstration Lessons Throughout the Year

Earlier in this chapter I suggested that the following demonstrations, most of which become classroom rituals and routines, can and should be taught early in the year. They are the keys to classroom management in the Literacy Studio. You'll find that many need to be repeated throughout the year to develop and maintain thriving literacy community and a smoothly functioning Literacy Studio. These should not be seen as teacher-driven lessons; students should be up and moving around the classroom, practicing the actual processes they will use throughout the year and later demonstrating for newcomers to the classroom and other students who haven't had experience with them. Fishbowl demonstrations in which one group of students reveals how a particular process works can be particularly effective.

- Independent problem-solving throughout the Literacy Studio

    - Where to find materials for reading, writing, and revising

    - How to gather in the Crafting—large group—area

    - How to transition to Composing (independent work) to focus on independent reading or writing

    - Responding (changing activities) to musical cues

    - What to expect and how to participate in an Invitational Group (small teacher-led group with focused instruction on a common need)

    - How to engage in conversation about a global question (see Chapter 8)

    - How to prepare and present a Reflection Session (share)/teach other readers and writers what you know

- How students can keep track of their thinking about texts in a notebook using a wide range of written, oral, and artistic tools including, but not limited to, sticky notes and advanced organizers (double-entry journals, timelines, Venn diagrams, sketches, etc.)
- How to work toward class reading and writing goals and how to set individual goals toward which students work during Composing
- How to put the classroom back together after a Studio
- How to collect ideas and experiment in a writer's notebook

- Book selection

  - When and how to select a new book
  - Familiarity with the collection (i.e., a book frenzy)
  - Where and how to access new books—how books are categorized in the room
  - How to recommend a book to another reader
  - How to make wise selections with respect to all eight factors that make a text readable for a particular child, beyond level

- Book clubs and small discussion groups

  - How to focus the conversation on a particular section of a book, a child's writing, and/or the application of a comprehension strategy
  - How to show the rest of the group that you are engaged
  - How to challenge another reader's or writer's perspective with cogent arguments
  - How to build upon one person's comments when you speak
  - Changing your perspective on the text based on another person's interpretation
  - How to effectively change the topic
  - How to pose questions and solicit others' responses
  - How to reflect on your group's discussion following the book club orally or in writing
  - How to decide, individually or with a group, how to take action in the world

- Keeping a writer's notebook

  - How to use a notebook every day to collect and experiment with ideas for writing

  - How to make notebooks the go-to spot for capturing an image, an overheard conversation, a quick thought, a photo, a question, an artifact or found object, a reminder . . . anything that *may* become fodder for writing

  - How to use notebooks to show that students can apply the concepts/goals as well as the intentions (goals they have set for themselves)

  - How to share and confer with peers around student notebooks

  - How to review writing in search of "gems" that may lead to more developed or published pieces:

    - Gems (Bomer 2010) are pieces of writing (even very short) that are deeply meaningful to the child, something that they find beautiful, surprising or that trigger an emotion—writers search through prior writing looking for words, phrases, sections that represent their strongest writing.

    - Students may choose the topics about which they write, or the teacher may ask students to apply a concept recently taught in their notebooks.

- Topic selection

  - Tactics to use when selecting a topic

  - Thinking through which genre might be most effective for the topic the child has in mind

  - How to mine topic ideas from the "gems" in a notebook

  - "Testing" a topic—sharing an idea with other writers to gauge their interest

- Interacting during Crafting and Composing

  - Turn and talk (rotating your body to face and briefly share an idea from the Crafting Session with a partner)

  - Jot and share—use a whiteboard to show your thinking during Crafting

- ◆ Quick check (a quick meeting with a partner to share progress on something both are working on in independent reading and/or writing—happens during Composing)
- ◆ Reading with a partner, aka buddy reading (reading a section of challenging text together to provide word level and comprehension support)
- ◆ Preparing for and setting reading and writing goals in conferences with the teacher
- ◆ Conferring with another student on a reading or writing goal

- Sharing your thinking

  - ◆ Adding thinking to an anchor chart
  - ◆ Sharing thinking during a Crafting Session
  - ◆ Sharing thinking during a Reflection Session (i.e., an open-forum discussion)
  - ◆ Thinking aloud about text

Part 3: The Canvases: Texts for Crafting Sessions

One of the great joys for many of us in teaching reading and writing is the stunning variety of beautifully written texts that serve as a student's guide to facts and ideas, the sound of gorgeous language, and the world beyond their schools and communities. Books spring to life when we discuss and interpret them and use them as fodder and mentors for writing. Using the brushes (teaching tactics) and paint colors (concepts children can apply to texts they read and write), our learning communities create rich and varied canvases that will differ from one year to the next. The interpretation of a book is different in the hands of each child who reads it. Children's writing is an important canvas and one of the most stunning representations of who they are, where they come from, and what they seek in life. It is because of the sparkling range of children's backgrounds, experiences, and beliefs that we see canvases in full relief, alive.

Most of us spend our careers purchasing and using children's books to delight and inform our students (and ourselves). We understand that texts of every type help students grow background knowledge (schema), which makes it easier to learn more complex information.

So many authors have written about the importance of using a wide range of children's books, the beauty and profundity, the insight and wonder offered in them; I won't try to match the compendium of their knowledge in this book.

I will not, however, miss the opportunity to add my voice to the chorus imploring teachers to immerse students in the diverse world including texts that focus on:

- race, racism, diversity, equity, and inclusion across all races
- issues related to Indigenous populations
- LGBTQIA+ (lesbian, gay, bisexual, transgender, queer and/or questioning, intersex, asexual, plus others) individuals
- gender diversity and expression
- identity
- stories of heroic actions by people of color *and* stories of everyday life in BIPOC (Black, Indigenous, and people of color) communities
- a range of perspectives on historical events
- the scientific world of wonder and discovery
- the aesthetic world including art, music, sport, and nature.

The extraordinary range of rich literature and informational texts available to students today should be accessible to all—all means all—students and that they should be able to not only see themselves but learn about the world outside their immediate reach through these texts. The diverse range of exceptional texts calls into question how, in the twenty-first century, we would find ourselves using poorly written texts, didactic nonfiction books, texts that have been "controlled for vocabulary" and level, or books that provide a narrow view of the world. Forty years into my career, I acquire well over a hundred children's books a year to build my own knowledge base and to use in the classrooms where I teach. Books are such powerful teaching tools, but I must remind myself, too, that reading aloud—no instruction, just immersion in a book—is in every student's best interest, no matter their age.

Of course, these books serve as mentor texts for young writers. We reveal the strategies and tools authors use to craft their exceptional books and encourage students to give them a try. I also want to remind you that the other critically important text you use for teaching writing is your own writing, crafted on your own first or publicly on a chart or document camera. Students become deeply engaged as they watch and contribute to a teacher's evolving writing in narrative and informational text. When teachers think aloud as we write, it gives students rare insight and access to the work of the writer's mind. We need to take a deep breath, get over the fear of writing in front of our students, and embrace the opportunity for success and struggle (the latter is often better fodder for learning) alongside our students. To do so breaks down all kinds of barriers students feel when they share their early attempts at writing.

Pulling It All Together

Sample Lesson Outlines That Incorporate Reading and Writing Strategies, Tools, and Standards

Let's return to our image of teachers as painters in a studio. Each of the following potential lessons incorporate state standards for reading and writing, strategies, and tools as I've described them. The lessons also integrate reading and writing and use texts by and about diverse people. They involve the careful selection of the brushes, paints, and canvases, as I described previously.

This is important: I wish I could use bold, twenty-eight-sized font that is underlined and italicized for this paragraph. In planning these lessons, my colleagues and I *began with a clear understanding of what the students need as readers and writers, what they are working toward, their intentions*, and then decided upon learning targets that integrated reading and writing. We chose our brushes, colors, and canvases for the lessons and *then, finally, lastly* looked at which standards to incorporate. Our hope was to move beyond methodical teaching of one standard followed by another and another to more meaningful learning for students, learning that incorporates the standards based on our observations of their needs. We wanted the image on the canvas to be vivid, engaging, and applicable to a wide range of literacy uses across the curriculum and for a long time to come. These lessons are not one-offs. Teachers spend days and sometimes weeks working side by side with students in Crafting Sessions and Invitational Groups and through conferences (see

Chapters 6 and 7) to ensure that they understand all the ways they can use these literacy tools going forward.

Sample Lessons

This section provides you with a wide range of potential lessons across the grade-level range, all of which integrate reading and writing and focus on a standard within the context of a strategy. Additional lessons are available online, see page ix. The long description of a single lesson in Chapter 4 and Figure 5.1 should provide background on what each of these lessons looked and sounded like in the classroom where the lesson was taught, but for length, I've abbreviated the lessons into a table (see Figure 5.2).

Let's start by looking at one of these lessons. In the first lesson in Figure 5.2, the fifth-grade teacher was concerned that students' writing was "all over the place." They had difficulty keeping their narrative writing focused and struggled to plan a piece. They "just write into their pieces and sort of make it up as they go along. They don't seem to have a main idea in their pieces." In conversation, she admitted that her students didn't consistently distinguish the most important ideas as readers—they could name one idea when it was offered as a multiple-choice option but weren't applying the standard in their real reading.

When we constructed the Crafting Session, we wanted to address both needs and to anchor our learning targets with a thinking strategy—determining importance—that will have staying power. The strategy (see the online resource Thinking Strategies and Writer's Tools) is an umbrella under which other learning targets, strategies, tools, and concepts fall. Students need to determine importance not just in literacy learning, but throughout their lives. The reach of this lesson extends far beyond the standards or any tests they might take—we're providing tools that readers and writers need. Integration helps students see that, whether they are reading or writing, they will construct more meaning if they focus on what's most important. For those reasons, the brush we chose (the teaching move) was thinking aloud, the paint color or concept was *how readers and writers make decisions about what matters most, to them and to the author whose text they're reading.* As writers, the tool was *how can writers reveal important ideas to their readers.* You'll notice that there is no mention of "main idea"—a concept that has always befuddled me. How can any text worth reading or writing have *one* main idea? Research does not support the notion that teaching main idea is helpful and, in my view, we should broaden our focus to the multiple ideas and themes in narrative text.

Figure 5.2 shows how reading and writing are integrated with a thinking strategy. Rather than reading through the entire table, find your grade level for an example of how you can create meaningful lessons that include standards, but are far more enriching and meaningful than a lesson that begins and ends with the standard. Complete sample lesson plans are available online. Keep the Crafting Session example from Chapter 4 (poetry with a focus on images and white space) and the think-aloud sample in Figure 5.1 in mind so that you can imagine the larger context and instructional tactics as you focus on your grade level's example. Focus on the third row: Crafting (the Lesson). That's where it all comes together.

Lesson 1 ▪ Grade 5	
Reading Standard	Determine a **theme** of a story, drama, or poem from details in the text, including how **characters in a story or drama respond to challenges** or how the speaker in a poem reflects upon a topic; summarize the text. Literature
Writing Standard	Orient the reader by establishing a situation and introducing a narrator and/or **characters**; **organize an event sequence** that unfolds naturally. Narrative
Crafting (the Lesson)	**Learning Target:** reading-writing connection Think-aloud focused on how readers identify what is most important to them in text and tools writers can use such as repetition and length to show their readers what is most important.
Thinking Strategy	Determining importance
Texts and Resources Used*	*Four Feet, Two Sandals* by Karen Lynn Williams and Khadra Mohammed

*Texts and resources were chosen to focus on a wide range of diverse texts.

Figure 5.2 Sample Lesson Outlines

	Lesson 2 ▪ Grade 4
Reading Standard	Explain how an author uses reasons and evidence to support particular points in a text. Opinion or Nonfiction
Writing Standard	**Develop the topic with facts**, definitions, concrete details, quotations, or other information and examples related to the topic. Opinion or Nonfiction
Crafting (the Lesson)	**Learning Target:** reading-writing connection Think-aloud with excerpts from the book (read aloud in its entirety the day before), *Nelson Mandela*. Focus on the global question (see Chapter 8): "Can nonviolent protests lead to solutions in social conflicts?" Discuss the question and then shift to discussing how readers can use a question to understand more deeply. The teacher also thinks aloud while writing to show how an opinion piece can start with a global question.
Thinking Strategy	Questioning
Texts and Resources Used*	*Nelson Mandela* by Kadir Nelson
	Lesson 3 ▪ Grade 3
Reading Standard	Describe **characters** in a story (e.g., their traits, motivations, or feelings) and explain how their actions contribute to the sequence of events. Literature
Writing Standard	Use dialogue and descriptions of **actions, thoughts, and feelings to develop experiences and events** or show the response of characters to situations. Narrative

*Texts and resources were chosen to focus on a wide range of diverse texts.

Figure 5.2 Sample Lesson Outlines, *continued*

continues

	Lesson 3 ▪ Grade 3, *continued*
Crafting (the Lesson)	**Learning Target:** reading-writing connection Global question: "How does conflict shape our reading, our writing, our world?" Write aloud (on a document camera or chart paper) to show how a character you're working on experiences external conflict. Think aloud about how conflict shapes a character, what you want your character to experience externally and internally. Speculate about how your character can change as a result of these conflicts. Read and think aloud in *Radiant Child* (first six pages) to focus on how the author uses conflict (internal and external) to show change in characters. Pause for a turn-and-talk. Use schema to recall well-loved texts where conflict shaped the character's actions, feelings, and beliefs. Read remainder of the book focusing on how the author uses internal and external conflict. Turn-and-talk: "What's your plan as a reader? What's your plan as a writer? (e.g., will you read with an eye to how conflict shapes change (internal or external) in a character or will you write conflict into your piece and show how characters change as a result?)"
Thinking Strategy	Schema
Texts and Resources Used*	*Radiant Child* by Javaka Steptoe
	Lesson 4 ▪ Grade 3
Reading Standard	Recount stories, including **fables, folktales, and myths from diverse cultures**; determine the **central message**, lesson, or moral and explain how it is conveyed through key details in the text. Traditional literature
Writing Standard	With guidance and support from adults, produce writing in which the **development and organization** are appropriate to task and purpose. Non–genre specific
Crafting (the Lesson)	**Learning Target:** reading-writing connection Think aloud about how readers make decisions about what's important *differently* in traditional literature than in contemporary literature. Writing focus: model a response to text (as opposed to original writing). How can we use written conversations or idea webs to capture important ideas in a variety of traditional literature? Eventual goal: create a response to text that has a clear organization and focuses on important ideas in a traditional text.

*Texts and resources were chosen to focus on a wide range of diverse texts.

Figure 5.2 Sample Lesson Outlines, *continued*

Lesson 4 • Grade 3, *continued*	
Thinking Strategy	Determining importance
Texts and Resources Used*	*The Royal Bee* by Frances Park, Ginger Park, and Christopher Zhong-Yu Zhang

Lesson 5 • Grade 3	
Reading Standard	**Ask and answer questions to** demonstrate understanding of a narrative text, referring explicitly to the text as the basis for the answers. Literature
Writing Standard	Use dialogue and descriptions of actions, thoughts, and feelings to develop experiences and events or show the response of characters to situations. Narrative
Crafting (the Lesson)	**Learning Target:** reading-writing connection Think aloud, focusing on questions that **cannot** be answered in the text to help us understand and empathize with characters. Global questions: "In what ways do authors spark questions in readers? Under what circumstances would authors spark questions that can be answered in the text, and when would they try to spark questions that cannot be answered in the text? What are some of the unanswerable questions we've discussed this year? Is it important to think about unanswerable questions?" Finish reading the text thinking aloud about questions provoked by *Dreamers* that cannot be answered in the text—questions that help us understand and empathize with the characters.
Thinking Strategy	Asking questions
Texts and Resources Used*	*Dreamers* by Yuyi Morales

*Texts and resources were chosen to focus on a wide range of diverse texts.

Figure 5.2 Sample Lesson Outlines, *continued*

continues

Lesson 6 ▪ Grade 2	
Reading Standard	Describe the connection between a series of historical events, scientific ideas or concepts, or steps in technical procedures in a text. Nonfiction
Writing Standard	Write informative/explanatory texts in which students **introduce a topic, use facts and definitions to develop points**, and provide a concluding statement or section. Nonfiction
Crafting (the Lesson)	**Learning Target:** reading-writing connection Think aloud in the chimp section, focusing on cause and effect—e.g., the chimp pokes hole in wood, finds termites to eat; the chimp fights with another chimp, resulting in an injury—model by creating a T-chart to show how what the chimp does ("behaviors and actions," column 1) lead to an effect ("what happens," column 2). Discuss as a whole group: Why do authors use cause and effect in their pieces? Is it an effective writer's tool? Why? Emphasize that students' informational writing will need to show cause and effect. Read and think aloud about cause and effect in the bonobo section. Read the section on humans. Think-aloud global question: "What actions do humans take (cause) that lead to negative effects on wildlife?" What evidence of a cause-and-effect text structure did students notice? What will they try as writers? Turn-and-talk: Introduce synthesis as the process of the reader changing their thinking as they read. Think aloud using synthesis in the gorilla and orangutan sections tomorrow.
Thinking Strategy	Synthesis
Texts and Resources Used*	*Ape* (chimp, bonobo, and human sections) by Martin Jenkins and Vicky White

Lesson 7 ▪ Grade 1	
Reading Standard	Read grade-level text orally with accuracy, appropriate rate, and expression on successive readings. Literature
Writing Standard	**Produce and expand** complete simple and compound declarative, interrogative, imperative, and exclamatory **sentences** in response to prompts. Non–genre specific

*Texts and resources were chosen to focus on a wide range of diverse texts.

Figure 5.2 Sample Lesson Outlines, *continued*

Lesson 7 ▪ Grade 1, *continued*	
Crafting (the Lesson)	**Learning target:** reading-writing connection Write aloud, pausing to think aloud about times when you have to revise your piece and how you know you need to revise. Model to show how to add, delete, and reorganize writing. Read or reread *Wolfie the Bunny*. Pause to think aloud about events or characters that confuse you. What can you do to resolve your confusion? Readers revise just as writers do. When and how do readers revise?
Thinking Strategy	Monitoring for meaning
Texts and Resources Used*	*Wolfie the Bunny* by Ame Dyckman and Zachariah OHora

Lesson 8 ▪ Grade K	
Reading Standard	With prompting and support, identify the reasons an author gives to support points in a text. Narrative nonfiction
Writing Standard	Use a combination of drawing, dictating, and writing to **compose informative/explanatory texts** in which students name what they are writing about and supply some information about the topic. Narrative nonfiction
Crafting (the Lesson)	**Learning Target:** reading-writing connection Write aloud to share information about a topic you're interested in. Model by talking about why you care so much about this topic and what you want your readers to know and understand after they read your informational text. Read *Wild Horse Winter*, pausing to think aloud about what Tetsuya Honda does to create a vivid setting and share information at the same time. After reading, discuss: "What is our schema for this author? What do we know about how she likes to share information with her readers? What information did she have to know to write this book?" Discuss: "What's your plan as a reader? What's your plan as a writer?"
Thinking Strategy	Schema for authors
Texts and Resources Used*	*Wild Horse Winter* by Tetsuya Honda

*Texts and resources were chosen to focus on a wide range of diverse texts.

Figure 5.2 Sample Lesson Outlines, *continued*

Notice: Each Crafting Session in Figure 5.2 assumes that students are already reading texts and writing in a notebook or possibly working on a polished or published piece. The assumption is that they will leave the Crafting Session to experiment with the strategy and/or tool in their own reading and/or writing when it fits with the reading and writing they're doing. See Chapter 6 for more information on how students make that choice.

Each Crafting Session in Figure 5.2 could be done as a longer, one-day lesson or spread across a couple of days as shorter lessons. Try not to separate all the focus on reading into one day and all the focus on writing on another day. Integrate the think-alouds on each day if you're spreading them out in shorter Crafting Sessions.

In this chapter, I hope you've seen how once you carefully select the brushes, paints, and canvas for your Crafting Sessions, there are an infinite number of combinations you use in a Crafting Session. Remember, your students' needs come first. The reading and writing learning targets, tools and strategies, the standards, the texts, and the teaching moves are assembled as a mosaic based on students' needs.

They work to apply what they've learned as readers and writers in Composing Sessions. Up next: How do we manage Composing Sessions in which students choose when to read, what to read, when to write, and what to write to meet class goals and their own goals? Composing is the beating heart of the Literacy Studio. Let's dive in!

CHAPTER SIX

The Heart of Literacy Studio

Independent Composing

> *The symbiotic relationship between reading and writing is a cornerstone of our individual intellectual journey and our educational system. We write as an act of self-expression. We read because language renders unto us the vitality of real and imagined experience.*
>
> —Marita Golden, *The Word*

Marita Golden is an award-winning novelist, nonfiction writer, distinguished teacher of writing, and cofounder of the Hurston/Wright Foundation, a national organization that serves as a resource center for African American writers.

Here's an idea for your next Crafting Session: read Marita Golden's beautiful quote above and ask your students what they think. Perhaps that's a bit much for seven-year-olds, but it captures so beautifully the relationship I'm trying to describe in this book. Ask the older students: What does a reader learn about writing? What does a writer learn about reading? Revisit those questions often. The twin vines of reading and writing we have long separated will begin to twist and grow together as you foster interdependence between reading and writing in your classroom.

This chapter focuses on the beating heart of the Literacy Studio—children reading and writing, speaking, and listening, and children deeply engaged and exercising choice in when and how to read and write, experimenting with the concepts you've taught, revising as writers, revising as readers. Composing is the setting in which the "symbiotic relationship between reading and writing" about which Golden writes emerges and thrives.

Take a moment to place yourself as an observer in your own classroom during a Composing Session. Can you see your students lost in the act of writing or reading? You have become temporarily obsolete (until your next conference) and time seems to stand still. The world around the kids seems to have disappeared; you see some engrossed in a novel, others delving into informational text to answer a pressing question, some are writing in their notebooks, experimenting with a writer's tool you've recently taught. You notice a pair of students collaborating on a project about the shrinking polar ice cap. You move among them, stepping over resources spread out on the floor, tiptoeing around students absorbed in their work—you notice that some are flowing back and forth between reading and writing. You shift into conferring mode, delving into conversations with kids about their most recent goals and intentions as readers and writers, their application of lessons you've recently taught. When the studio time is over and you interrupt, they look up almost like they must reorient themselves to time and place. They look around in something like bewilderment; they could have continued for much longer.

I join you in wishing this scenario was real more of the time. This chapter is about making those intense, productive, joyful moments commonplace. We'll start by tackling the question about what language to use in the studio and move into examples of primary and intermediate Crafting and Composing Sessions.

The Language of Literacy Studio

When I first experimented with Literacy Studio in my own and other teachers' classrooms, I assured teachers that it doesn't really matter what we call the different components of the model. You can call Crafting Sessions whole-group lessons; don't worry about whether you refer to independent work as a Composing Session or not. I've changed my thinking about the importance of the terms we use to describe the components of Literacy Studio. I do encourage you to adopt these terms as a way of signaling to yourself, your colleagues, and your students that we need to change the way we view our time as language users and to describe more precisely what we're doing in different phases of that time.

In Crafting, we study the craft of the reader and the writer; we delve into writer's strategies and tools, *and* we attend to our thinking about and discoveries in text. Standards are integrated into our discussions about new approaches we might try as readers and writers; we are craftspeople, designing, building, reshaping, rethinking, rebuilding—together. We're engaged in active discussion about what readers and writers do, and we pause to admire the beauty of language and the impact it has on us, intellectually, emotionally, in our beliefs, and in the actions we take in the world. Together.

In Composing, we are drafters and revisers of meaning. We actively compose meaning as readers, attending to our thinking, our discoveries, and our reactions to text, interpreting and deciding what ideas are worth remembering. We actively compose meaning as writers, sculpting the words on the page and offering them to an audience we hold close as we write. We go back and forth between reading and writing over and over. We consider how, as writers, we might cause our audience to react with joy or despair; we think, as readers, about how the authors we read manipulate our thinking and emotional responses. We *compose* with language no matter how we're using it. We experiment and are dissatisfied; we try again.

Why is it that we see adult reading and writing as intricately connected, but don't apply the same lens to students' work? I'm composing; I'm reading and writing; and there is a very, very fine line between them. My eyes are on text, my mind is immersed in ideas, only my hands behave differently, and even that difference is minimal. I'm composing.

As a perhaps too obvious example, as I compose this chapter, I'm surrounded by texts—books by authors I admire and intend to quote and research on the teaching of reading and writing. I toggle back and forth between reading and writing frequently; I sometimes read for several "writing" sessions as a way to fill my mind with the philosophical and practical pulse points I hope to strike. I reread what I've written many, many times and often delete huge sections. I place the deleted portions in a file I euphemistically title "Later," but there is very little chance those portions will ever see the published light of day. They didn't work, but I would have no way of knowing that if I weren't constantly in a revision mindset, rereading, rereading, rereading. Of course, I have immersed myself in reading, naturally I go back and forth between periods of reading and writing; it simply wouldn't make sense for me to do otherwise. Why is it that we see adult reading and writing as intricately connected, but don't apply the same lens to students' work? I'm composing; I'm reading and writing; and there is a very, very fine line between them. My eyes are on text, my mind is immersed in ideas, only my hands behave differently, and even that difference is minimal. I'm composing.

For these reasons, when we begin the transition from a reader's and writer's workshop to Literacy Studio, I believe that we need to use a new language to describe our work. In my experience, children love the idea of composing in a working studio, a beehive of engaged learning, a place where they have many choices and must be accountable. I've thought long and hard about the terms I've used to describe each component of the studio. I hope you'll consider the symbolic and practical impact of using the terms *Crafting*, *Composing*, *Invitational Groups*, and *Reflecting*. Simple and layered with meaning.

What Is Composing?

Before we dig into a couple of real-world Composing Sessions, let me give you a bird's-eye view.

Composing: Who, What, Where, When?

Everyone in the classroom engages in independent reading and writing during Composing, but it isn't always quiet, individual work. Students frequently engage with other students in inquiry projects, book clubs, responsive writing, and peer conferences. The teacher observes (at least five minutes in every Composing Session), confers with individuals, and meets with small, needs-based groups, which we'll call Invitational Groups (see Chapter 7).

The hope is that the Composing Session will be a time when students lose themselves in the process of reading and/or writing much like the description at the beginning of this chapter. If we seek engagement, offering choice is key. Students may also choose where to work in the classroom as long as they can focus. They monitor their engagement level and can make a change to reading if they aren't engaged in writing and vice versa.

Let's talk a bit more about offering students the choice of whether to read or write. I've found much deeper engagement when I offer students the choice of when to read and when to write. Because most Crafting Sessions focus on reading *and* writing, students choose to work on either or both to apply the learning target from a recent Crafting Session. Not to worry! They don't get to make all the choices every day. Students are expected to apply roughly equal time to reading and writing so if a child chooses to write on a Wednesday, generally speaking, the expectation is that they will read on Thursday. In addition, there are times when the teacher wants all students to work on a class goal as readers first or focuses on a goal that applies primarily to writing and asks the students to write for a day or two in a row or the reverse. Of course, you are the decision-maker; choice can be rescinded if a student is, shall we say, in need of a bit of focus!

My students loved the idea of choice, but also became overwhelmed with the choices I gave them. So even though they were eager to try it out I needed to pull back the choices that were available and build them back in little by little. This idea of choice also opened the doors for them to explore passions and different writing styles. They discovered what they enjoyed writing about and how they enjoyed writing. I encountered more authentic and genuine writing and I could see the growth. I could hear their voice and personality in their writing.

—Karla Contreras, second-grade teacher, Milagro Elementary School,
  Los Angeles, CA

Initially, many teachers ask students to choose whether they will read or write for the first half of the Composing Session and then ask them to switch at the check-in midway through. As they grow more comfortable, students are allowed to switch between reading and writing day by day and even week by week, especially for students who might be working on a long-term inquiry or writing project. The latter is rarer; usually students switch by day, one day writing and the next reading, but in both cases, working on the class goal that emanated from a recent Crafting Session.

Composing Sessions comprise approximately two-thirds of the Literacy Studio, so if Literacy Studio is 120 minutes, the Composing Sessions take approximately ninety minutes. Some days when a Crafting Session is longer, Composing Sessions are shorter; on other days students will have longer Composing Sessions with little or no Crafting Session.

Ninety minutes can be a long time for young students, especially early in the year for most, so we should plan for students to interact frequently during Composing. This can be in the form of quick turn-and-talk interactions, book clubs, interactive writing (like written conversations), and/or peer conferences. We should also build in check-in moments. These are brief teacher-initiated pauses in Composing Sessions and are timed to give everyone a chance to refocus, perhaps to switch from reading to writing or vice versa. The teacher may ask students to join them in a central location for a standing meeting, to reflect on their progress with another reader or writer, or to quickly record their thinking about their work and progress toward goals. Composing is not one long, silent, uninterrupted stretch of time. To be engaged, students must know their purpose and interact frequently with others.

Teacher Goals and Student Intentions

In Literacy Studio, students' independent work is goal driven; students are usually working on a whole-class goal that stems from a recent Crafting Session (see Chapter 5). Importantly, though, it's important that we understand the student's *intention*—what they would like to try as a reader and writer. An intention is a personal goal they have set with a teacher in a conference or Invitational Group. As the school year progresses, students take more responsibility for their own intentions—new strategies, tools, and conventions (spelling, punctuation, grammar) they would like to work on.

Let's talk for a moment about other types of goals and intentions. I find it useful to differentiate between surface structure (word learning) and deep structure (meaning making) work during Composing (Keene 2008). For example, a first-grade writer may be working to combine clusters of letters into words by using spaces between words in their writing (a surface-structure

Karla Contreras and Second-Grade Students

goal). This is a personal intention; many children in the class may have already mastered "wordness." Simultaneously this child's class is working on the thinking strategy *schema* (background knowledge) as readers and writers (see Thinking Strategies and Writer's Tools [available online, see page ix]). Strategies are deep structures or meaning-related goals.

Often young children are eager to use surface structures such as fluent oral reading, spelling, punctuation, and so on, and they become intentions, something the child seeks to do. Of course, we need to monitor students' reading and writing carefully and encourage them to work on particular surface-structure goals as the need becomes apparent. I'll say more about word learning and surface structures later in this chapter.

What about record keeping for all of this? The goal is to ask students to keep track of most of their work during Composing Sessions, yes, even the littlest ones. We may launch the year with more teacher-driven records, but we transition as quickly as possible to student record keeping for the time spent in reading and writing in Google Sheets or Google Docs, in their note-book, on index cards at their table. The important point is that students keep track of how they spend their time—even little ones. We also want children to keep track of their progress toward goals. Many Literacy Studio teachers ask students to keep "thinking notebooks" in which students develop seeds for their writing projects (see Chapter 5) and record thinking about text. Teachers keep detailed conference notes and frequently review student work to assess progress toward goals. (See Appendix 2 for student and teacher record-keeping ideas).

Following each Composing Session, students move into Reflecting (see Chapter 8) for an opportunity to share progress toward goals and intentions and "teach" other students what they have learned to do as readers and writers.

Planning for Composing

We discussed planning in Chapter 3, but it bears repeating that most of the planning (see the planning wheel in Appendix 1) focuses on what the students will do during the Literacy Studio time, what we're calling Composing. Recall that Crafting Sessions make up only about one-third of our weekly allotment for the Literacy Studio. When planning a unit, and then on to a weekly plan, and a daily lesson, our focus is on what we want students to experience during Composing Sessions.

In this section, I would like to share an example of the planning process, and later the Crafting Session and Composing Session I shared with a first-grade teacher in Fort Osage, Missouri. A bit of background—I have been privileged to work with this extraordinary school district, east of Kansas City, Missouri, for a half dozen years or so. In Fort Osage, teachers use the Literacy Studio model, and instructional facilitators have designed the curriculum to integrate reading and writing. They incorporated the Missouri state reading and writing standards, but they took a very innovative approach to building their curriculum. Instead of creating a relentless pacing guide that enumerates the standards, directs exactly when and how they should be taught, and creates a system whereby teachers check each off a list after "assessing students' mastery" in an endless sequence of disconnected, irrelevant content and instruction designed primarily to boost test scores on invalid and unreliable assessments, regardless of students' needs (am I making very clear how I feel about a lot of American curricula? I don't want to be too subtle!), the team at Fort Osage used common sense, knowledge of learning research, and children's needs to create their curriculum. The curriculum is dynamic, changing based on teachers' feedback and new research, but the outcome provides teachers with a flexible template in which they can integrate reading and writing with an emphasis on *thinking, the strategies* children need as readers and writers. Teachers bring their creativity and knowledge of students' needs to weekly lesson planning rather than following a published program with a script.

In the fall of 2019, I was looking forward to working with a first-grade class in Fort Osage, and the teacher, Janelle Keith, and I were trading emails as we planned for our time in her classroom. Her first email started with a yawn emoji and listed these two Common Core State Standards (CCSS) (National Governors Association Center for Best Practices, Council of Chief State School Officers 2010) as concepts she hoped we could address during my visit:

> Read grade-level text orally with accuracy, appropriate rate, and expression on successive readings. (CCSS, 1. R. F. 1. 4)

> Produce and expand complete simple and compound declarative, interrogative, imperative, and exclamatory sentences in response to prompts. (CCSS, L. 1. 1. J)

I agree. Doesn't every first grader just long to produce and expand complete simple and compound declarative, interrogative, imperative, and exclamatory sentences in response to prompts? And what about their chomping-at-the-bit eagerness to read grade-level text orally with accuracy, appropriate rate, and expression on successive readings? It's the stuff of first-grade dreams, isn't it?

It's not that we don't value sentence variety in writing and prosody in reading—of course we do. The question is how to build Crafting Sessions that inspire kids to *want* to use these skills and how to create a climate in Composing time that supports students' experimentation and *gradual* success with applying them in meaningful contexts, in an age-appropriate way. We have to start by thinking about two very simple questions:

- What do we want the students to *try* as readers and writers?
- How do we want the students to *feel* as they build proficiency in the concepts?

We start by visualizing what we want children to experience as readers and writers during Composing using these standards; then we work backward to build the Crafting Sessions that lead students closer to that ideal. We need to imagine how we want kids to feel when they use the skills successfully—yes, *feel*. We want children to reap the internal reward for reading and writing fluently. We want them to experience the moment when they think to themselves, "Yes! I did it the way great readers and writers do it." We want them to see, for example, that it's fun to use short and long sentences, to embed a question into their writing occasionally, and to make a statement that shows how strongly they feel about something; we want them to view these constructions as *tools* a writer uses, and it is all possible for them as writers. We want them to feel the joy of reading aloud a page of a book they love in a way that sounds "just like the author would read it." It is all possible for them as readers.

Second, we need to create conditions in the classroom where students know that writing and reading are rarely "finished" the first time around; we want them to experiment, try again, make meaning progressively clearer as readers and writers. We want them to fall in love with trying again—we want to create a climate that values *revision*. Both goals are much larger and longer lasting than merely showing application of a standard.

We begin by thinking about the Composing time—the time when students do the work of readers and writers. We want to hone our awareness of what each child is already doing well related to the standards and forgo a one-size-fits-all instructional approach. Importantly, let's look for kids who have begun to experiment with sentence variety, exclamation points, and questions in their writing and make their successes public. Let's find students who love a page in a book so much that they have practiced it until it sounds as beautiful when they read it aloud as it does when they hear their teacher read it.

In the Fort Osage English language arts curriculum, the Missouri state standards are grouped under an umbrella thinking strategy (Keene and Zimmermann 2007), in this case, *monitoring for meaning*. This gave my first-grade colleague and me a way to create meaningful, contextualized Crafting Sessions and, importantly, a vision for Composing (independent work they would do) from standards that are, well, less than inspiring. We wanted our Crafting Session, that day and always, to be just that—inspiring—and we wanted kids to head off to Composing with drive to create and clarify meaning.

With the overarching idea of monitoring for meaning in mind, we started by taking a look at the goals we have for readers and writers who monitor well (Figure 6.1). We wouldn't dream of teaching *all* of these goals to first graders, but based on Janelle's knowledge of their needs and interests, we decided that the work children would undertake in the next couple of weeks would focus on the goals in bold in Figure 6.1.

We concluded that both the standards on which we intended to focus, our concepts, and the monitoring meaning goals are ultimately about *revision* and the capacity to resee is a gift.

Monitoring Meaning and Comprehension

Readers

▶ Readers monitor their comprehension during reading—they know when the text they are reading or listening to makes sense, when it does not, what does not make sense, and whether the unclear portions are critical to overall understanding of the piece.

▶ Readers can identify when text is comprehensible and the degree to which they understand it. They can identify ways in which a text becomes gradually more understandable by reading past an unclear portion and/or by rereading parts or the whole text.

▶ **Readers are aware of the processes they can use to make meaning clear. They check, evaluate, and make revisions to their evolving interpretation of the text while reading.**

▶ Readers can identify confusing ideas, themes, and/or surface elements (words, sentences, text structures, graphs, tables, etc.) and can suggest a variety of different means to solve the problems they have.

▶ Readers are aware of what they *need* to comprehend in relation to their purpose for reading.

Figure 6.1 Monitoring Meaning and Comprehension

continues

> ❯ **Readers must learn how to pause, consider the meanings in text, reflect on their understandings,** and use different strategies to enhance their understanding. This process is best learned by watching proficient models "think aloud" and gradually taking responsibility for monitoring their own comprehension as they read independently.

Writers

> ❯ Writers monitor during their composition process to ensure that their text makes sense for their intended audience at the word, sentence, and text level. **They revise and eventually edit to ensure that their writing is meaningful.**

> ❯ **Writers read their work aloud to find and hear their voice.**

> ❯ Writers share their work so others can help them monitor the clarity and impact of the work.

> ❯ Writers pay attention to their style and purpose. They purposefully write with clarity and honesty. They strive to write boldly, simply, and concisely by keeping those standards alive in their minds during the writing process.

> ❯ Writers pause to consider the impact of their work and make conscious decisions about when to turn a small piece into a larger project, when revisions are complete, or when to abandon a piece.

Figure 6.1 Monitoring Meaning and Comprehension, *continued*

Primary (First-Grade) Composing Session

The pieces for our time in first grade were coming together. We set the following learning targets for students:

- Children will continue to grow in monitoring and revising their writing to include a wide variety of sentences and ideas to enhance meaning.

- Children will monitor and revise their oral (and silent) reading to reflect what they understood from texts, revel in making even small changes to clarify meaning, and experience the moments when important ideas come into focus when they read.

Do you see how the standards are embedded in the concepts, but the concepts are more relevant and meaningful? The strategy, monitoring for meaning, gives us a way to contextualize what might otherwise be a disconnected series of lessons on prosody and types of sentences.

Ultimately, we hoped that children would begin to think of themselves as artists, dabbling with language, and see themselves as agentive and powerful monitors and revisers of thinking in writing and reading—that's a different outcome than asking whether they read fluently aloud and use different-length sentences. As we planned, we wondered together why children often emerge from primary grades viewing revision as something tedious and onerous. We were determined to do our best to prevent that with these young children.

When I used to teach literacy, it was very separated. I would teach a skill and just expect the students to know how to do it without any practice. Students rarely had time to read during the day. Using the Literacy Studio, I teach a skill and then the students get to practice as a reader or a writer. They have a choice in their learning, and I have seen so much more growth. I printed out small calendars for them to keep track of when they read and when they wrote so they don't spend too much time just reading or just writing.

—Emily Lapp, fifth-grade teacher, Fire Prairie Upper Elementary, Fort Osage, MO

The Crafting Session

We began the Crafting Session with a short demonstration using a piece of my writing about flying. Before I showed my writing, I talked animatedly about how I never tire of the view from an airplane window; I spoke about seeing the land, but also loving to fly above heavy cloud cover and how occasionally one sees another airplane streaking below or above in another direction and how much I love to witness that—assuming that few others on the plane have noticed what I just saw. It feels like great insider knowledge.

Then on the document camera, I shared a few sentences I'd written ahead of time in a dull series of declarative sentences devoid of energy, sentences that reflected little about my excitement when I fly.

Me: I love to fly. I like to sit at the window and look out.

I read the sentences in a tone that illustrated my lack of enthusiasm, and the students immediately noticed that my writing didn't match the tone of my oral description of the experience.

Student: You didn't make it sound as good in writing.

First graders being the nexus for honesty and feedback in the known universe.

Student: Yeah, it was boring when you read it.

Great, they were already monitoring. They were paying attention to the differences in my oral and written language. I named what they were doing and wrote "monitoring for meaning" on chart paper.

We had been paying close attention to how the writing of several children sounded when they read it aloud, and I called on one of them to share his experience.

Me: Jackson, I've heard that you know how to make revisions, changes in your writing, to make your writing sound more like how it would sound if you were telling the story. Can you help me out?

Jackson: Yeah, you have to add some stuff.

I looked at him quizzically.

Jackson: You have to add the sentences about the part you love the most.

I loved that.

Jackson: Like you didn't say anything about seeing other planes.

We were off! I won't go into much more detail about his part of the lesson but suffice to say I quickly reworked the two sentences and added a third that detailed what it's like to see another airplane streaking across the sky. I used the word *streaking*, I made sure that the sentences varied in length, and I used an exclamation point. I told them that to revise, as Jackson and I had done, was one of the greatest feelings a writer can have because a writer can see their writing becoming clearer and more aligned with the excitement they feel about the topic. I reminded them that paying attention to how your writing sounds, knowing that it reflects your emotions, and knowing if it is clear enough is called monitoring, and as I handed the baton to my colleague, I added the word *revision* next to the word *monitor* on the chart paper and added an arrow pointing from *monitor* to *revision*.

> **Janelle:** So, we know that, as a writer, you're always monitoring your writing, trying to decide if it makes sense, if your audience will find it engaging, and if it shows your feelings about the ideas. Mrs. Keene forgot to show us how excited she is when she flies. She wasn't monitoring at first and you guys helped her so much. Once she monitored and paid attention to how her writing sounded and how it made you feel as her audience, she revised—she made important changes in her writing to make it more meaningful.
>
> The same is true for readers. When you're reading and you feel confused or something doesn't make sense, you know the author didn't want you to feel that way, right? So, the voice in your mind that talks to you when you read says, "No way! That doesn't make sense. What can I do?"

She paused and asked them to turn and talk to a partner about how readers can clarify meaning, once they've monitored and know that something doesn't make sense. They had discussed these issues earlier in the year but hadn't called the process monitoring and revising.

Janelle had read the enchanting book *Wolfie the Bunny* (Dyckman and OHora 2015) twice earlier in the week and asked the children to recall how they had puzzled over why a family of bunnies might adopt an abandoned baby wolf. She reopened the book.

> **Janelle:** Do you remember how confused we were here? We know that wolves actually eat rabbits in the wild and we couldn't understand what the bunny mom and dad were even thinking when they brought Wolfie home!
>
> **Student:** Yeah, he's just going to eat them!
>
> **Janelle:** Right. We were really worried about that, and the author didn't tell us why a family of bunnies would adopt a wolf.

Janelle shared two other spots where there had been questions and confusion on the first reading and reminded them that when they reread certain sections and when they reread the book, those ideas became clearer. She used the words *monitoring* and *revising meaning* several times during the Crafting Session.

The talk was lively, and the moment had come for the transition into Composing. I popped back into the lesson.

Me: OK, everyone, you know that you have a big decision to make right now. We've been talking about how writers and readers monitor, how we pay attention to times when what we're writing and what we're reading doesn't make sense or could sound much better and then we revise.

I pointed to the chart paper.

Me: Now it's your turn to think about how you want to monitor and revise in your own reading and writing. Soon, we'll add your examples to this chart. For now, show me with your hands if you're going to start off today with reading (I mimicked opening and closing a book with my hands) or show me if you're going to practice monitoring and revising as a writer. (I mimicked writing with hand movements.)

About six students showed that they intended to write. Some of the students mimicked both reading and writing; others didn't indicate for either reading or writing. They were just getting used to having this kind of choice in how they spent their Composing time. I saw that I needed to be more precise.

Me: If you're choosing to write today, you'll go back to the little book you're working on, and you'll reread it (probably aloud). You can monitor to see if there is a part that doesn't make sense or could be more exciting or interesting. Then you can choose to revise, to change the part that doesn't make sense. You can add something like I did a few minutes ago or you can take a part out. Would anyone like to try monitoring and revising as a writer today?

We had a solid eight hands and, using my well-loved staggered-start send-off, I sent those students off to begin.

Me: Now what about it, readers? Who wants to try reading one of the books in your book boxes (probably aloud) and listen so carefully, monitor, to see if

> it sounds beautiful or funny or cool, just like the author intended it to be.
> If it doesn't, then as a reader, you would revise, reread it until it sounds
> just like the author is reading it.

Most of the students seemed to understand, and I sent them off to get their book boxes and to settle in around the room. Two students remained. I knew one was an English learner and I didn't know the other. I trusted that she remained on the floor because she didn't yet know what she was going to do. I gestured to join me as I stood up to walk around the room. I love to take students along on my observation time. We move around the room, noticing and describing what other readers and writers are doing. Occasionally, if I sense that one or two students might have difficulty getting engaged in their work, I'll invite them to walk and observe with me. It's my way of pointing out the positive behaviors around the room and giving them an idea of what engagement looks like. After a few minutes, I ask them if they're ready to jump in for themselves, and it usually leads to engaged reading and writing.

I walked with these two around the room noticing aloud what others were doing.

> **Me:** Oh, see how cool it is that Jovani is already adding a part to his writing?
> He's monitoring (I made a face to show that he wasn't happy with what he
> had written) and now he's changing it.

We watched Jovani erase and add a few letters to his writing and continued our observation tour. I pointed to two boys who were reading their writing aloud to each other.

> **Me:** Oh, wow, look at that. Oh, you guys! I so hope that those two are going to
> give each other feedback the way Jackson did for me when my writing
> sounded boring.

Of course, I said this well within hearing range of the two—they heard it and went back to reading aloud. Triumph (I hoped)!

I won't say 100 percent of the time, but very nearly, these little observation walks help children see how others are working; they see exactly what they're doing in a very concrete way, and they're off to get started. If engagement starts to wane later in the lesson, I grab a couple of kids and repeat the observation.

Following our little walkabout, Janelle and I decided to begin conferring with the pair of students who were reading their writing aloud to each other. I was excited to see them trying to monitor and revise together, but I wanted to ensure that it stayed productive and led to revisions in their writing.

I took one last look around the room before sitting on the floor with the boys. Thanks to Janelle's yearlong work in helping them understand what it feels like to be engaged readers and writers, there were only two children "in transit," moving around to pick up materials or resettle elsewhere in the room. They didn't need to be told, again, that Janelle and I were beginning to confer and that we would be unavailable to others; we trusted that if problems arose, they would take steps to solve them. They had heard and experienced this dozens of times.

Our single most important goal for Literacy Studio was being realized— the children were engaged in reading and writing independently. That does feel great!

Conferring

An In-Depth Look at a Conference with Canyon

I'd like to focus on a conference in some depth—exactly what was said *and* what I was thinking—because conferring is where we spend the vast majority of our time during Composing. In addition, this conference is characteristic of early literacy conferences in which there are two or more readers and writers working together. In Chapter 7, I'll share much more information about conferring in a Literacy Studio, but as we did with Crafting in Chapter 5 let's do a deeper dive into this conference. I am giving you the unedited version here, good, bad, and ugly! It's all right here.

Following the observation, Janelle and I settled in next to Canyon and Tamir, who had been reading their writing aloud to each other earlier.

> **Me:** Hi, you two! Do you have time for a conference? We'd like to hear how you started Composing time today. How did you decide to read your writing aloud to each other?

Tamir responded without looking up from his writing.

Tamir: I'm trying to make this better.

He was trying to erase words from his little book about his dog's escape. He was so intent on his revisions at that moment, I decided to turn to Canyon, who seemed a bit more distracted.

Me: Canyon, what can you tell us about what you and Tamir were doing to support each other as writers?

Canyon: Um, we, he, he had to change it. (Apparently in reference to Tamir's writing.)

Me: Great, what did you say to him that helped him to monitor and revise?

Canyon: Um, well, I said what kind of dog is it and how did he escape?

Me: Wow, how did that help him as a writer?

Canyon: I don't know, I think he added that stuff.

Me: Well, what about your writing, Canyon?

Canyon: It's OK.

These are the last words I wanted to hear after a Crafting Session on revision and monitoring!

Me: It's OK, huh?

It wasn't a brilliant start to a conference, but I was stalling for time, trying to figure out what I could say next. C'mon, it's not easy to confer with a first grader who thinks his writing is OK!

Me: Have you read your writing to Tamir yet?

Canyon: Nope. He's doing something now.

Me: Well, when two writers are working together, they both get a chance to read their writing aloud and get the other writer's feedback, right? While Tamir is finishing his revisions, why don't you read your piece aloud to us?

I wonder now if asking Canyon to read to us was a misstep. I inserted two adults into the partnership, and I think it might have been better if we had encouraged them to go back to reading aloud—this time it would be

Canyon's turn. I did want Tamir to revise, though, and I was afraid he might forget his idea if he waited until after Canyon shared. Toss up . . . The one thing I know for sure is that there is never only one right way to approach a conference. I was in it now and I needed to follow through with Canyon.

Canyon perked up a bit. He read from his little book about a birthday party he had recently attended. He had used markers to make colorful illustrations on all but the last page of his little book, and he set about describing each of them to us.

> **Canyon:** OK, this is when we got there; this is the velociraptor I gave him; this is the cake; this is the other presents . . .

I was now feeling more confident in the direction we could take.

> **Me:** Wow. You're the kind of writer who likes to start with the illustrations and let them tell the story.

I always want to affirm what the young writer or reader is doing in the context of building their identity as a language user: "You're the kind of writer who . . ."

> **Canyon:** Yep.

Canyon was a man of few words. At this point, he was looking around for his markers and realized they were at his table. He looked a little desperate.

> **Me:** I'd like to invite Tamir to join our conversation. Tamir, are you in a good place to stop revising and listen as Canyon reads his writing to you?

> **Tamir:** Yeah, just let me . . .

His voice trailed off. I made a mental note to tell Tamir that he's the kind of writer who is intent on making revisions; I knew then that I wanted him to share, not his story necessarily, but how it felt to be a writer intent on revising when we came to Reflecting time. Often, I discover great things students are trying in a conference and I invite them to share it during Reflecting.

> **Me:** OK, Canyon, Tamir is getting ready to listen to you share your writing.

Tamir looked up and Canyon described the illustrations exactly as he had to us moments before.

> **Tamir:** I was at that party too.

Janelle: OK, great, you can help Canyon monitor his writing and make revisions just like he did for you?

Tamir: Well, it's just pictures.

Janelle: Say more.

Brilliant move.

Tamir: What if it goes to the Room 112 Writer's Shelf?

He referred to a shelf in the classroom where children categorized their books and made them available for others to read. Bingo!

Me: What do you mean, Tamir?

Tamir: If it goes to the shelf, and somebody reads it and they weren't at the party, they won't know.

A great example of monitoring.

Me: OK, so you're monitoring, Tamir. You're saying that if Canyon wants others to understand his book . . .

Tamir: He has to have words.

Me: I see. So, Canyon, what do you think about Tamir's suggestion?

Canyon: I like to make the pictures.

My mind flashed back to the learning target we were working toward—using a variety of sentences in writing—*my* goal for these students. Tamir had opened the door for me to encourage Canyon to add sentences. I did brief battle in my mind between leading him in that direction but I just couldn't go there. Canyon's words, "I like to make pictures," were crucially important if we're to truly follow the child's lead in a conference. I decided to help him develop the little book into which he had already put so much time. He was excited by it; he was telling a story. How might I push him to develop his story using pictures and still learn something about making our writing more meaningful? That seemed to me to be the most important focus, for now. This is the difference between our goals and their intentions. We needed to ensure that Canyon moved toward using a variety of sentences in his writing, but today, his *intention* was to "make pictures." Whenever possible, I'm going to try to follow the child's intention, even if it means putting my goal on a brief hold!

Canyon reminded me—again—of this simple statement in teaching: it is important to be flexible. We are often so driven by our own sense of urgency, by our need to tick concepts off our list, we lose track of the child's intention. Canyon wanted to "make pictures" and this, too, is important. In fact, it's more important than getting to instruction on the teacher's goal. He is far more likely to be engaged when he is in hot pursuit of his own intention, and engagement is crucial. Janelle will get back to the need to add words to the pictures, as will, as I come to think about it, every other teacher for the rest of Canyon's education. I made a mental note to talk to Janelle about the possibility of hosting an Invitational Group (see Chapter 7) for Canyon and others who used illustrations as their primary way of writing books.

Me: OK, I understand that. Lots of authors write wordless picture books.

I gestured to a nearby shelf with boxes of wordless picture books.

Me: Are you saying that you want this book to be a wordless picture book?

Canyon: Yeah.

We were hardly surprised, but I could see ways to focus on monitoring and revising as well as learning about story structure through wordless picture books.

Me: OK, that's great, Canyon, but here's the thing. Author and illustrators of wordless picture books still have to monitor and revise to make sure their books make sense. In fact, it may be even harder to make sure that your reader really understands the story if you don't use words, but I love wordless picture books and if you want to make one about this birthday party, there are a couple of things you need to do. First, we want you to share the story with Tamir again now that he knows it's going to be a wordless picture book. He'll have to look and think carefully to make sure that someone who wasn't at the party could understand the book just by looking at the illustrations, right?

Tamir (nodding): You didn't put anything in about the pizza.

Canyon: OK.

Canyon reacted well.

Me: The other thing I want you to think about, Canyon, is how the authors and illustrators of other wordless picture books use illustrations to tell a story, a whole story. Do you have any favorite wordless picture books?

Canyon: I love *Chalk*! (Thomson 2010)

The children had already had immersion experiences in wordless picture books, and Janelle quickly grabbed *Chalk* for Canyon. I was delighted—what a great mentor text. There is complexity, humor, a clear story structure, and, best of all, he already loved it.

Janelle: We'd like for you to reread *Chalk* and think about all the things Bill Thomson, the author-illustrator, does in this book to help readers understand the story without any words.

Canyon was all about digging back into *Chalk*.

Me: Canyon, I want you to read *Chalk* at least a couple more times and really monitor, that means pay attention to, the way he shows the order of events in his book. I'd like for you to think about what he put first and why, what he included second . . . And please really focus on the last pages of his book. What does Bill Thomson do to let the reader know it's over? What will you do as a writer? How will you revise your book to include illustrations that will show your readers how cool the birthday party was? OK?

He was already digging in and didn't answer. I took that as a good sign. Both boys were so intent on their work that we decided to circle back to Tamir when he had completed his revisions, but Janelle asked him if he would be willing to share in Reflecting time about the monitoring and revising he had done. He was more than agreeable. "I'll teach!" he said without a moment's hesitation. This is a classroom where children frequently teach their classmates, a concept we'll dig into in Chapter 8.

We heard Tamir telling Canyon what to add to his wordless picture book; we'll leave it for another day to help these writers understand that every single detail they remember doesn't necessarily need to be included in the book. We made a note of the fact that we need to nudge Canyon closer to including sentences in his writing but didn't regret that we had followed his excitement toward a more developed wordless picture book in lieu of forcing him into adding sentences.

Perhaps he will find enough momentum in his book to publish it in two forms, a wordless picture book and a book with words, to describe that birthday party.

We left knowing that Tamir and Canyon had an idea about monitoring and revising in writing and that they had goals to lead them forward.

A Quick Conference with Jacey

We moved around the room to observe other students and were thrilled to see most of them sustaining reading and writing. We discussed whether to rescue Cassie, who was wandering around a bit and stealing furtive glances in our direction, and, we thought, making it clear she was all about getting us to confer with her. I must admit that I was ready to succumb, but in talking it through with Janelle, we thought better of it. If we conferred with her at that moment (though her wandering was driving us crazy), she would have learned that she could get us any time she wanted by being disengaged. We were pretty proud of ourselves when we turned away and went to confer with Jacey. And sure enough, when I looked up the next time, Cassie had switched from reading to writing and had reengaged herself—no small feat for someone who is six!

Janelle: Jacey, are you working on monitoring and revising as you read?

I loved the way she saved time by going straight to the point. We weren't here to chat about her books; we were here to see how she was progressing toward the goals we had set in the Crafting Session.

Jacey announced proudly:

Jacey: I'm reading *I Am the Dog I Am the Cat*. (Hall and Moser 1994)

Janelle: I love that you picked that book up, Jacey. We've read that one since the very beginning of the year, haven't we? There are so many amazing words. I'm curious, sweetie, how have you been monitoring and revising as a reader this morning?

Jacey: I've been knowing when I get stuck.

Janelle: Great! That's a big part of monitoring. Can you show us a place where you got stuck?

Jacey flipped back a few pages to the illustration that shows a baby sitting on the cat. She laughed.

Jacey: I don't get this word.

The word was *acquaintance* in the phrase "making the acquaintance of babies."

> **Janelle:** Hmm, that's a tough one. Do you remember how it sounded when I read it aloud and do you remember what was happening at this point in the book?

A great question—there is a lot of challenging (and beautiful) vocabulary in this book, and she was working to get Jacey off the fixation on a word to the larger meaning. Jacey knew exactly what was happening.

> **Janelle:** OK. Let me just tell you the word and then it will be easier to go on. The word is *acquaintance*.

She read the page and they talked briefly about what the word meant.

> **Janelle:** So now you know what *acquaintance* looks and sounds like, Jacey. Did you get stuck anywhere else?

Immediately, Jacey pointed out another word she couldn't remember or read. Janelle made a great move here—we could have been focusing on identifying words all day.

> **Janelle:** So, it seems like you're the kind of reader who is very tuned in to the words you don't know and that's an important way to monitor and revise, Jacey. Would you like to learn another one?

Jacey was game.

> **Janelle:** There is a difference, Jacey, between monitoring at the word level— you're already good at that—and monitoring at the idea level. You're ready to learn what that means.

Jacey wasn't following.

Jacey: Idea?

> **Janelle:** Exactly! Monitoring and revising meaning at the idea level means that you're thinking about the big ideas, the important parts the author, in this case Donald Hall, wants you to know as you read. So, what are the big things, the big ideas, that Donald Hall wants you to know in this book?

She slid the book away from Jacey to help her think about her question without the immediate distraction of the book.

Jacey: Um, that . . .

There was a long pause, quite uncomfortable for the adults, but we did a great job (a lesson learned after many missteps) waiting, restating the question, and helping her feel as comfortable about taking her time to think as we could.

Janelle: I love the way you take your time to think, Jacey. I'm asking you to think about the big ideas, the parts Donald Hall wants us to remember for a long time, and you're taking your time to think about it. That's great.

Often, it's just a matter of giving time and occasionally restating the focus.

Jacey: Oh! He wants us to know whether we like dogs or cats. I like cats! We have a cat . .

It was tough, but Janelle interrupted before we got into a long story about Jacey's cat.

Janelle: OK, so Donald Hall is trying to help his readers decide whether they like dogs or cats. What are the other important ideas?

As the conference continued, it became clear that Jacey wasn't seeing the whole of the book; she wasn't attuned to the bigger ideas in *I Am the Dog I Am the Cat*. What did the author want us to think about when reading this lovely book? We played "my turn, your turn" with Jacey because we sensed that she needed, as many first graders do, to move beyond monitoring at the word level and she needed us to think aloud a bit more before she was able to grasp the concept. We asked Jacey if she wanted us to go first or if she'd like to go first—never fails, they want us to go first, and it's not surprising because what they're really saying is, "Hey, you two, I need more instruction on this concept." So, Janelle and I shared a couple of our big ideas about the book, one of which is that Donald Hall wants us to see how different dogs and cats are by pointing out the funny quirks about each and that he wants us to see what is so lovable about both and to show how independent they are, each in their own way.

Janelle: Your turn, Jacey!

Jacey: Um, I think that the big idea is . . .

Another long pause ensued.

Jacey: I think the big idea is that you're supposed to know what is good about dogs and cats.

She announced this in a way that revealed her pride in breaking into a whole new chapter as a reader. She could monitor for big ideas as well as words that threw her off. She could monitor for what she *did* understand as much as what she didn't understand. It was a pretty big breakthrough and we left her with a choice about whether to reread *I Am the Dog I Am the Cat* and think about more big ideas or whether to think about what big ideas she wanted the readers of her books to think about when they read her writing.

Jacey said what every teacher longs to hear:

Jacey: Can I do *both*?

Janelle: Well, er, let's see, shall we let her tackle both, Mrs. Keene?

Me: Gee, I guess so, I never thought of that, Mrs. Keith.

We conferred with two other children that morning and circled back to Tamir for a "flyby" conference just to check if he was ready to share his monitoring and revising process with the rest of the class during Reflecting.

We held a brief check-in—a standing meeting right at the midpoint of the Composing Session.

Janelle: OK, everyone, come to the Crafting area, but don't sit down and get comfortable. We just want to check in to see what problems you've solved on your own and remind you that if you're not feeling really engaged, you can switch to work on the same goals in the form you haven't been using, either reading or writing.

Cassie raised her hand.

Cassie: I got bored.

Janelle: OK, Cassie, how did you solve that problem?

Cassie: Well, OK, I just switched to writing.

Janelle: Fantastic problem-solving!

Phew, I was so glad that we didn't bail her out when she was wandering around the classroom.

Janelle and I were pleased that the children were so engaged for so long and mentioned that to them. Everyone got the wiggles out and headed back to reading and writing.

When Reflecting time rolled around, we were also delighted to hear Tamir share his revisions with the group and Janelle teased the idea that tomorrow Jacey would be teaching about a brand-new kind of monitoring that she learned how to do today.

I looked at the clock—unbelievable! Ninety minutes had elapsed. It feels so good to have kids and teachers working side by side. One lesson, one goal—monitor and revise as readers and writers—was enough to sustain these *first graders* for that long. They could have gone longer.

Intermediate Composing Session

We've taken a deep dive into an intermediate Crafting Session in Chapter 4, and this one in a primary Composing Session, so I'd like to conclude this chapter with just a short peek into an intermediate Composing Session. There are so few differences from the Composing time in Janelle's classroom, but I do want to focus on a couple.

The Crafting Session, in a fourth grade, focused on generating questions about the beautiful book *Nelson Mandela*, written and illustrated by the extraordinary Kadir Nelson (2013). You can see the learning targets by revisiting Figure 5.2, lesson 2 on page 105.

Similar to our first-grade send-off, we sent the readers and writers off to work, and we spent a few minutes observing the students. Those who were reading were doing so in a variety of genres, as were the writers.

There was an inquiry group in the middle of their work, though. Five students had become fascinated with Nelson Mandela in prior class discussions and hadn't yet seen the Kadir Nelson book. They couldn't wait to get their hands on it and were rereading it as we observed. I stopped by to ask, *"What problems are you working together to solve?"* In my mind, there is a huge difference between *participating* in a group research process and truly *collaborating*, which implies that there is at least one complex problem to be solved. I asked the question in that way to find out if students were clear on what the problem to be solved was and to let them know that I wasn't there to help, I was there to witness their work.

In a short aside, I have become concerned in recent years about the degree to which we see learned helplessness in children. I wonder if we trust them enough to solve their own problems in academic and social settings. I have tried to curb my instinct to jump in and say, "Have you tried . . . ?" or "Why don't you think about . . . ?" and to say instead, "I'll be so interested to see how you solve that problem. Let me know, won't you?" as I turn and walk away. I want them to know that I believe they can address most issues that they face. I want them to build agency, to think, "I'm the kind of kid who can deal with this!"

While the other fourth graders around them delved into using questions as readers and writers (see Figure 6.2; in bold for the focus for this classroom's study), the Nelson Mandela inquiry group had a problem alright. They had generated so many questions about Mandela that they were overwhelmed and unsure about where to start. A flurry of sticky notes lay around them, and I saw more on their Chromebook screens.

Figure 6.2 is the list of strategies we reviewed to select the (bold) concepts for our fourth-grade lesson.

Asking Questions

Readers

▶ Readers spontaneously generate questions before, during, and after reading.

▶ Readers ask questions for different purposes, including clarification of meaning, making predictions, determining an author's style, content, or format, and to locate a specific answer in text or consider rhetorical questions inspired by the text.

▶ **Readers use questions to focus their attention on important components of the text.**

Figure 6.2 Strategy Focus for Intermediate Questioning Unit

continues

▶ **Readers are aware that other readers' questions may inspire new questions for them.**

Writers

▶ **Writers compose in a way that causes the reader to form questions as they read.**

▶ **Writers monitor their progress by asking questions about their choices as they write.**

▶ **Writers ask questions of other writers to confirm their choices and make revisions.**

▶ **Writers' questions lead to revision in their own pieces and in the pieces to which they respond for other writers.**

Figure 6.2 Strategy Focus for Intermediate Questioning Unit, *continued*

Student: We have so many questions and we can't decide which ones to answer.

Me: Hmm, that's tricky. What have you thought about so far?

Student: One of us should just pick.

Me: Well, that's one way, and I think you'll ultimately have to decide for yourselves. You're going to have to prioritize, right? There are a lot of good questions, and you want to make sure that your audience will understand what you've all decided is most meaningful for them to know about Nelson Mandela. Have you ever tried a pyramid to decide?

They hadn't.

A decision pyramid can be used with sticky notes, index cards, even scraps of paper to build from the bottom up to identify the most important elements of any decision. I suggested that the students group the questions that might lead to information that provides some color commentary (not essential but illuminating) and then work upward toward the top three or four questions that they use to decide together about the focal questions for their inquiry. I love these pyramids and use them all the time with kids. Inevitably, and this is exactly what happened that day with the Nelson Mandela inquiry group, students find a way to combine similar questions, delete less relevant ones, and argue (in a productive way) about the most essential questions and content for their audience. These students dug in, and when I circled back to them later, they were collaborating (eureka!) and had created a pyramid with six (OK, a few too many, but they had the right idea) sticky notes as the foundation of the pyramid and were discussing which three to eliminate from a very top-heavy point of the pyramid.

There is a lovely rhythm to Composing Sessions once they are up and running; I discovered this in the early days of the Literacy Studio in my classroom. Once I decided to release myself from the tyranny of the clock by integrating most reading and writing lessons, there was much more time to confer, and I felt far less urgency about accelerating my conferences and moving on to the next reader or writer. I must watch myself because I do get very caught up in conferences—kids are just so endlessly fascinating, right? But I know now that there will be time to confer and to pull Invitational Groups (read on) because we're not caught up in an endless series of transitions to minilessons and small groups. The kids get into the rhythm too. They're not working on using three different types of sentences, they're working to monitor and revise to make their meaning clearer, which may mean greater sentence variety. There is a world of difference between the two and the latter leads, not surprisingly, to much greater engagement.

Kids need to feel that they are working toward worthy goals that will make a real difference to them in being able to do what they want to do as readers and writers. They are natural language producers, to be sure, but we need to help them see that there is an important reason to try out the strategies and tools we teach. With worthy goals, the luxury of time to read and write, and the right to move back and forth between the two as we do in the world outside the classroom, I've found that they rise to the occasion. Imagine the joy when you look out across your classroom and see that engagement for yourself.

CHAPTER SEVEN

Composing

How It All Comes Together

Let's imagine that you've decided to create a Literacy Studio in your classroom. Where to begin? We've talked about several moving parts thus far, so in this chapter we'll look at a step-by-step plan for getting started with Literacy Studio as well as adaptations for students with learning differences, children who are learning English, and very young children. We'll also dig into what makes for a great Invitational Group and the fine art of conferring with students in the Literacy Studio.

First, a brief review . . .

COMPOSING IS:

- An extended time each day for children to immerse themselves in reading (challenging and interesting texts in a wide variety of genres) and writing (in little books for young writers and then writer's notebooks, collecting and gathering short pieces they may choose to develop into more formal pieces later). They apply what they have been taught in Crafting Sessions and Invitational Groups and create new goals alongside their teachers and on their own!

- A time when students experiment with what has been taught in reading and writing. That said, it is important to remember that a student may not be working as a reader or a writer on a piece in which they can

142

immediately apply what has been taught in a Crafting Session. We don't want to force inauthentic reading or writing merely for the sake of showing immediate application of a tool or strategy. With effective record keeping (see Appendix 2), we can encourage a child to table the tool or strategy until they have a more logical context in which to apply it.

- An opportunity to choose whether to read and/or write. The child has to do one or the other, depending on their energy and focus and depending on which area the child feels they can best apply what has been taught. They make this choice based on recent learning targets and goals for readers and writers as well as their current intentions in reading and writing. Children are expected to keep track of the time they spend in reading and writing and must devote equal time (on that day or later in the week) to focusing on the other.

- An opportunity for children to select text that is interesting to them and appropriate, given their goals as readers, and to select writing topics about which they are passionately interested. Students apply what they have recently learned in Crafting Sessions and Invitational Groups and realize their intentions as writers.

- A time for individual children to meet in conferences with their teacher to show application of deep- and surface-structure strategies (in reading and writing) recently taught and to set ambitious new goals toward which they will work. Students talk about their intentions as readers and writers, and teachers help them create intentions using tools and strategies that have been taught, or in some cases, new learning the teacher shares during the conference.

- A time when children read and write independently while their teacher confers and hosts Invitational Groups. When students are not in an Invitational Group, they are reading, writing, and/or discussing books and writing with peers. There is no need to invent other activities to keep them busy!

- An opportunity for children to meet in pairs and small groups to discuss their books and writing. They discuss their application of goals and recently taught deep- (meaning-based) and surface-structure (word-level) strategies in reading and writing.

- A time for children to meet in pairs and small groups to apply speaking and listening learning tools and strategies taught during Crafting Sessions or Invitational Groups. Composing is an active time when students share, discuss, and seek feedback from their peers. There are opportunities each day for quiet work and for interaction within each Composing Session. For example, children may meet in book clubs and/or writers' groups to discuss books they have read in common and tactics they are using as writers. Or they may confer with each other about their reading and writing.

- A time to plan (with the teacher in a conference or with other students) what a student will share and teach others during the Reflection time. Reflecting time is the time when one student's learning becomes public for all.

Composing is the studio in the Literacy Studio! Think back to the artist's studio image we discussed in Chapter 5. This is where the wonderful messiness, the experimentation, the revision happen. And, importantly, there is real and important learning going on every day in Composing. Not only are students working to apply the concepts they have learned through Crafting Sessions, but they are also focused on their intentions, what they really want to learn and try as readers and writers. Composing Sessions provide us with the golden opportunity all teachers seek: to differentiate our instruction much more effectively.

It's important to know that there is a tone, a culture, that is pervasive in Composing. It's not only about kids reading and writing and teachers conferring and teaching in small groups; it's difficult, but I'll try to capture that elusive feel. In Composing, children are deeply engaged in independent work (see Essential Conditions for Literacy Studio [available online, see page ix] for conditions that enhance that engagement). They read and write with intensity for long periods of time. It doesn't start out that way; teachers help students build energy and engagement for independent work by beginning the year with short periods of time for Composing and building to longer periods.

Literacy Studios are characterized by a sense of urgency—children are ready to apply what they have learned in Crafting Sessions and Invitational Groups. They are especially eager to work on their own goals/intentions, usually two—one that they share with the rest of the class because the teacher has provided instruction on it (the concept that applies to reading and writing) and one that they have set for themselves or in collaboration with their teacher. They work in texts that are challenging to them, at the conceptual level as well as in text complexity. They write to apply what they have learned from instruction and from scrutinizing the work of authors they admire.

Modesta Urbina and Third-Grade Students

In Composing, you'll see and hear indications that rehearsal and revision are very important. Children experiment with new challenges as readers and writers, taking risks and spending a substantial amount of time rereading and rewriting. A quick aside: My colleague and friend, Chris Hall (2021), has just published the most extraordinary book on revising in writing. Wow, where was this book when I was in the classroom? Chris was probably in preschool! In a Literacy Studio as well as in Chris' classroom, children dive into reading and writing because they feel independent and *trusted* to make the right choices; they know it is up to them to choose the right text to read and writing topics, and when they encounter problems, they know to attempt to solve the problems independently first.

The only way I can capture the interactions among students is to describe a sort of camaraderie. Children in Literacy Studio classrooms are so excited to share their insights with other children in small-group discussions, book clubs, and writers' groups in which they react to each other's work. Of course there are days when it all falls apart—impending snow day, assemblies, the day after Halloween and Valentine's Day! It doesn't always work well for an artist in their studio either! But it is a studio. It feels like the epicenter of energy for literacy learning. My words are inadequate; you simply must experience it for yourself.

Do you have a sense of what matters most in Composing Sessions? Great, read on. Next up, I'm going to suggest a three-step plan for launching your

Literacy Studio. The steps have steps, so it's a bit more than a three-step plan, but hang in there with me. This is going to make a huge difference in your literacy instruction.

Launching a Literacy Studio for the First Time

1. **Design a unit.** Before you take on any structural or scheduling changes in your classroom, sit down with teammates or with the best company in the world—you—and make some decisions about your first integrated unit of study.

   a. **Content:** Complete this equation: your students' needs as readers and writers + reading standard + writing standard + thinking strategy = integration! What? This isn't a math book. Let's try this. Start with a good look at your students' work and the observations you've made as a teacher. What are their most immediate needs as a group? Then look at the standards and curriculum you're asked to teach in your state or school. Scan through the reading and writing objectives and ask yourself this question: Which standards or curriculum objectives *seem to fit together* and *what thinking strategy connects them*?

   For example, let's just look at a couple of third-grade standards. If you are focused on your state's version of CCSS standard RI 3.2 (National Governors Association Center for Best Practices, Council of Chief State School Officers 2010), "determine the main idea of a text; recount the key details and explain how they support the main idea," connect the writing standard that best matches that objective. For example, writing objective W 3.4 asks that students: "With guidance and support from adults, produce writing in which the development and organization are appropriate to task and purpose. (Grade-specific expectations for writing types are defined in standards 1–3.)" Perfect! Your instructional focus is on ways that readers make decisions about what is most important in an informational text and how writers signal to their readers that an idea is very important when writing informational text (see "Determining What Is Important in Text" in Thinking Strategies and Writer's Tools [available online]). Don't worry about a "perfect match" between the reading objective and the writing objective. Just play around with some possible combinations!

Here's another example. Think about RL 3.3, the standard in which children are asked to: "Describe characters in a story (e.g., their traits, motivations, or feelings) and explain how their actions contribute to the sequence of events." The writing correlate might be standard W 3.3: "Write narratives to develop real or imagined experiences or events using effective technique, descriptive details, and clear event sequences." You might choose to link these two objectives as part of a focus on schema (relevant prior knowledge; see Thinking Strategies and Writer's Tools online). You would select a stack of texts to use for think-alouds that show how authors use their schema to develop believable, interesting characters. How do believable characters help a reader understand fiction more effectively, and how, as writers, can students develop characters that are believable and interesting? The possibilities are endless!

Of course, standards aren't the only (nor often the best) source for content in your unit. In Chapter 5, I proposed that effective teachers draw from the needs students demonstrate for next steps in instruction as well as the strategies and tools we discussed—you won't always find those in standards documents. If, for example, a student wants to create tension and suspense in their writing (a tool from Thinking Strategies and Writer's Tools) you can identify mentor texts that provide relevant examples and discuss ways to create tension and suspense with the student in a conference or with others who have the same intention in an Invitational Group. We know that contextualized instruction is most effective, and there is no greater context than a student's expressed needs.

b. Instruction and practice: Use the planning wheel I introduced in Chapter 3 to sketch out three or four weeks. (I know I proposed it as a tool for daily planning, but it works great for unit planning too.) The teams of teachers with whom I work draw a planning wheel on large chart paper and sketch out our unit plans right on the wheel. Use the Composing section of the wheel to dream about what you want your students to experience and try as readers during this time. Will they read and write in a particular genre, or would you like for them to experiment with the concepts you teach (and their own goals/intentions) in several genres, getting a feel for how readers and writers determine importance in narrative, poetry, and nonfiction? Think about how you'd like your students to put new learning into action as writers. Then use the Crafting space in the wheel to list the concepts (standards, strategies, and tools) you hope to address in the unit. Don't go crazy here—fewer concepts taught in great depth over a long period of time and applied in a variety of texts = learning. What conversations do you imagine in Crafting Sessions and conferences about how students make their meaning ever clearer as writers? Which texts will you use?

c. Build your stack of mentor texts, diverse texts that represent windows, mirrors, and sliding doors (Bishop 1990) for children, and texts that your class just plain loves and returns to time after time. List them in the margins of the planning wheel.

d. Reflection: Think about global questions—you may want to skip to Chapter 8 for more information on global questions. These are questions that will help students think about the world beyond your classroom. Jot down a few and get ready to capture others during the unit—they will emerge through conversations you have with students.

Don't worry about getting every detail down—you know it's going to change once you see how students react—just sketch out the big ideas you want to share in Crafting Sessions. You and your team can build a weekly plan as you move through the unit.

2. **Structure your studio.** Some teachers have an uninterrupted block of time for Literacy Studio, others aren't so lucky (see Chapter 3 for more scheduling ideas). It doesn't matter. Just think about the $\frac{1}{3}$, $\frac{2}{3}$ rule. You get $\frac{1}{3}$ of the weekly literacy time for Crafting Sessions, Invitational Groups (see page 163), and Reflection (Chapter 8). That $\frac{1}{3}$ can happen in any configuration imaginable—you might end up with a longer lesson one day, shorter ones through the rest of the week; you might host Crafting Sessions at the end of the Composing time. Be flexible. However, if it feels more comfortable to start with a set schedule, try this one, but remind yourself that one of the keys to a successful Literacy Studio is flexibility. I've italicized the most crucial elements in the schedule.

   a. Crafting Session (twenty minutes, give or take), in which you think aloud in reading and in writing. This is the whole-class time in which you all apprentice to great readers and writers. It's the time to huddle together to think about the work students long to do. You'll think aloud and model the concepts—standards, strategies, and tools for readers *and* writers—but the hope here is to build a community of learners who are digging into important things they want to try as readers and writers. As always, encourage students to share what they're learning with other students in turn-and-talk sessions.

b. Composing time. We're starting the school year with less time and moving toward thirty to forty minutes for grades K–2 and forty-five to sixty minutes for grades 3–5, during which *students choose whether to read and/or write.*

  i. Time to confer with students (try starting with three to five minutes each) as everyone else reads and writes. If a child is reading when you arrive, focus on their reading intentions or reading goals for your classroom, but incorporate insights about how their work might apply to writing and vice versa. *Focus on the child's intention* as well as on how they are going to put concepts taught in the Crafting Session to work in their reading or writing.

  ii. Check-in (five minutes within the Composing schedule). Pull the students together into a standing meeting or just speak to them wherever they are about what they're discovering about themselves as readers and writers, what's going well, who might want to switch from reading to writing or vice versa. Stand and stretch a bit and back to reading and writing!

c. Reflection (ten minutes). Using the global questions you built into your unit plan, ask students to reflect on discoveries and insights about their reading and writing that day.

d. Invite students to share what they learned to do as readers and writers that day.

e. Jot notes about the needs you observed and wish to address the next day.

3. **Take stock.**

a. Take some time to *observe during the Literacy Studio.* What do the students need? Who needs reminders to move back and forth between reading and writing? Who seems to be most engaged? What conditions (see the online resource Essential Conditions for Literacy Studio) can you emphasize to enhance engagement?

b. Take a moment after school or at home to review your observation and conference notes and the students' record keeping. Revise your plans to ensure that your work the next day will be as responsive as possible for kids.

c. Formulate a plan for tomorrow. What will your focus be in the Crafting Session? Will there even be a Crafting Session? Do you need to call an Invitational Group? With whom do you want to confer?

That's it—my three-step/sixteen-step plan for getting started! Easy peasy, right? Maybe not quite easy peasy, but worth sticking a toe in the water, or diving in headfirst if you're anything like me—remember the spring break of *no snow*? Sometimes I dive in and nick my head on the bottom of the pool, but I rarely regret the dive. It's easier in a way to just tackle it all at once rather than starting with, for example, integrated Crafting Sessions, but of course that's another way to try it. Some teachers with whom I work launched Literacy Studio with Composing and simply offered students the choice whether to read or write on that day and built out from there. Wherever you start is the right place to start!

It's All About Differentiation: Diverse Learners, Conferring, and Invitational Groups in Composing

The Literacy Studio and Diverse Learners

I'm often asked about how the Literacy Studio works for children with learning differences and children who are learning English. I'll begin to answer that question here and we'll dig into it again as we discuss Invitational Groups and Conferring later in this chapter.

The Literacy Studio model is predicated on differentiation. It is built around the idea that children need to spend long and growing periods of time in independent work, reading texts that are appropriate for them and writing on topics of their choosing. The time for Composing will necessarily be shorter early in the school year but needs to expand as children engage for longer times in books and writing. As students are engaged in independent work, Composing for longer times, teachers are free to confer and meet with small, needs-based groups, what we call Invitational Groups. For children who are learning English and those with learning differences, this level of differentiation is crucial.

Unfortunately, we see too many children with learning differences trooping down the hall to pullout interventions where the instruction they get is not tied to instruction in the regular classroom and a great deal of time is lost in the transitions between classrooms. Although differentiated special education services and English support are crucial for some students, it can feel like they get a whole lot of instruction with very little time to practice—to read and write independently. As we know (Allington 2011; Harvey et al. 2021) volume matters—students need to read a lot and write a lot to improve. Students working in Literacy Studios have the time they need to read and write and the differentiation they need through your conferences and Invitational Groups.

So how do kids spend time reading when they're not matching voice to print yet, when they aren't yet able to read the books they enjoy? Volume

still matters for these children. The good news is that they can spend very productive time working with books that you've read aloud and discussed, especially if you've read the book two or three times. They can follow the story through pictures, read words they recognize, and retell as they go. And yes, many will need to spend time with predictable and decodable texts as they work toward reading fluency.

We know that recorded books (when children follow along with the actual book in their hands) are very helpful, particularly if they listen and follow along multiple times.

Today we have an extraordinary range of beautiful, wordless picture books that are engaging and help children build knowledge of narrative text elements. I know teachers who find that printed song lyrics of familiar songs are a huge boost for very young readers, children with learning differences, and children who are learning English. It's important to have the song lyrics in the student's heritage language and in English, permitting the student to learn the song in two languages. Books in which children can apply translanguaging are critical (España and Herrera 2020).

Partner reading can be helpful, particularly with a partner whose approximations are a bit more advanced. Most importantly, children need and deserve books in their heritage language; we need to keep adding to our classroom and school libraries. More books—I'm pretty sure I'm preaching to the choir on that one!

Repeated reading—finding an excerpt from a text that a child loves, copying it and encouraging them to practice reading it aloud until they sound "just like the author"—is another great option. I find myself using echo reading a lot with the students we're describing.

I turn echo reading into a "my turn, your turn" game in which the student chooses a part they love, you read it, then they read the same sentence or passage, repeating the process for as long as necessary. We can launch all these options through conferences or in Invitational Groups.

For writers who are just learning, we know that listening carefully to the sounds they hear in a word they wish to write and then encoding the letters (or an approximation of the letters) is incredibly important. In fact, writing is the best phonics practice a young child can have! Rather than telling a child how to spell a word, we invite young children to write what they hear, at least until they can decode predictably.

Making little books (Ray and Glover 2008) gives young children and those who need additional support the opportunity to create and "publish" a book with pictures and words that has a beginning, middle, and end. Because the books are, well, little, children tend not to be as overwhelmed as they might facing a blank notebook page or screen.

We can invite children with learning differences to dictate their work if necessary, and we can encourage children to tell their story or share their information through their own illustrations. I suspect we worry too much when young children, those with learning differences, and those learning English want to illustrate most of the time. Of course, we need to encourage them to add words as they're able, but illustrations can be a powerful way to help children create and elaborate on their stories and share the information that is most important to them.

The children we're discussing need a great deal of oral language practice as well. There is almost no way to overemphasize the importance of frequent oral language interactions among children and between children and their teachers. It's great to expand a rudimentary sentence a child has shared with you by recalling what they said using more complex syntax and more sophisticated vocabulary than they used. I develop these ideas much more in *Talk About Understanding* (2012).

Here are a set of principles I try to keep in mind when considering my approaches with children who have learning differences, very young children, and children who are learning English:

- First and foremost, create space for discovering the stories and identities of students of color. Make a wide range of materials available that center their languages and lived experiences.

- Invite families to be part of your classroom. Build relationships with parents and community members to ensure that children learn to value their own and other children's culture.

- If students leave the classroom for intervention, language, or special education support, coordinate as much as you can with the provider to ensure consistency in instruction—to the degree possible, advocate for push-in models.

- Employ visual supports, photographs, iconography, anchor charts, and so on as much as possible.

- Learn about and use translanguaging pedagogy.

- Plan on shorter, more frequent conferences.

- Meet with them at least twice a week in Invitational Groups. Remember that Invitational Groups may be more frequent early in the school year and until children can spend longer periods of time in independent work.

Composing is the opportunity for students to find deep engagement and meaning in the work they do. So, what makes Composing work smoothly? The refrain "It's all about differentiating" means it's all about conferring and hosting Invitational Groups!

Conferring

I have argued earlier in this book and will repeat here that conferences are the lifeblood of any version of reader's or writer's workshop and certainly are in the Literacy Studio. I'll also risk repeating myself to remind us that our central role as teachers is to know our students well, to build lasting relationships with each of them, and in so doing to differentiate for their learning and emotional needs. Conferring is the process of coming to know our children more intimately, of building reciprocal trust, and of plotting their learning path alongside them. I understand the challenges related to finding time to confer; that's why the Literacy Studio is such an important new way to look at how we structure time. When our lessons are integrated, when we're talking about reading *and* writing in nearly every conference and Invitational Group, we are liberating ourselves from the need to teach two lessons, confer with students about reading and writing separately, and teach small groups of writers and, later, readers. The Literacy Studio gives us (much) more time to confer. The important question, always, is how can this reader/writer reach beyond their current work?

What Does a Literacy Studio Conference Look Like?

These are only suggested steps for a conference. Keep in mind that although we are oriented toward goal- and intention-driven work, we want the conference to be informal, celebratory, and authentic. Generally, teachers confer in the student's workspace, not at the teacher's desk. If you approach a child who has chosen to read at that time, proceed into a reading conference and vice versa for writing, but don't hesitate to ask the child to switch to either reading or writing if it has been several weeks since you've conferred in that area or if you are eager for the child to demonstrate what they have applied in either reading or writing.

Try to confer with primary-aged children once a week; some intermediate children can work for a couple of weeks between conferences, but rules are made to be broken. Don't let equal be the obstacle; you will need to make decisions about which children need shorter, more frequent conferences and which will benefit from less frequent, more in-depth conferences.

NINE STEPS TO GREAT CONFERENCES

1. Take the child's temperature; how are they feeling, what do you notice about nonverbal signals and behaviors? Give some thought to how you'll accommodate the child's current social and emotional dispositions toward reading and writing.

2. Check on progress from the class goal and prior individual intentions—take careful notes. If age appropriate, invite the child to take notes on the conference as well. Listen to the child's perspective on their progress toward goals and intentions—take careful notes. Conferences should focus on what the child has to say rather than on what we have to teach.

3. I often confer using the book I read aloud that day (or earlier) if the text the child is reading or what they are writing isn't conducive to the concept I'm teaching or their goal.

4. Remind them about the learning targets the class is learning and inquire about how they are working toward the class goal or if their current reading and writing doesn't permit authentic application of the class goal; make a note about when, and in what context, they might try it. We use a combination of the record-keeping forms you see in Appendix 2 to keep track of the class goals on which I'll eventually need evidence of proficiency.

5. Ask them to read aloud *only* if your focus is on understanding their word learning or take a running record.

6. Be explicit about how the strategy or tool discussed in a conference can be generalized beyond the current context; make the link between reading and writing explicit. Help the child understand the relevance of their goals to progress as a reader and to thinking about the world outside the classroom. The conversation revolves around authentic issues, topics, and skills readers and writers will use going forward. Don't be afraid to teach in a conference!

7. Point out what the child is doing that is new for them as a reader or writer. Ask the child to point out what they are trying and what they would like to try next; what's their intention?

8. Invite students to share new insights during Reflecting Sessions (see Chapter 8) if appropriate.

9. Leave *each* conference with a clear direction; invite the child to describe the goal or intention in their own words to ensure that both of you have a record of the goal.

Teaching and Assessing Concepts in Conferences

Let's revisit our earlier definition of learning targets, which include concepts, standards, goals, and intentions.

- **Learning Targets:** New learning, including writer's tools, reading and writing strategies, concepts, and standards for students to apply as readers and writers following instruction at the whole-group, small-group, or individual level. Learning targets may not be immediately applicable to the reading and writing the student is doing. The teacher keeps track of new learning (anchor charts, class thinking notebooks) and encourages students to apply learning targets when appropriate in their reading and writing; all students should apply what is taught when it is relevant to their reading and writing (unless they already demonstrate the use of the tool or strategy).

  Learning targets should, whenever possible, align with the students' intentions. For example, rather than asking a student "How are you using dialogue in your writing?" because you taught it today, let's ask "How does our learning target, dialogue, from the Crafting Session fit your intention?" What if the child is reading and writing informational or opinion text? We have kept track, on anchor charts, for example, of several class goals, any one of which might be helpful at a given time. We need to ensure that the goal aligns with the student's intention—what they are trying to do as a reader and writer. We're pulling from all the strategies and tools we've been teaching over time and asking what fits now. Yes, they need to show application of the learning targets; the question is when?

Let's take a closer look at the difference between goals and intentions:

- **Teacher Goals:** Learning targets from any instruction often become goals for the group. These can be suggestions (or requests) that a teacher makes to encourage a student to try the learning target in their reading and/or writing. Goals may stem from review of student's work or instruction in Crafting Sessions or Invitational Groups; they relate to what we want all students (or a small group of students in an Invitational Group) to apply independently. Ideally, our goals are supplemented or replaced by students' intentions as the year goes on.

- **Student Intentions:** The hopes a student has, what they are trying to work on as a reader and writer in a text or written piece, the impact they are working to create in their writing, the ways they are working to understand more deeply in their reading. Intentions can become goals the student creates in the short or long term to accomplish something in a particular text or piece of writing.

  One of our aims in each conference is to generate an individual intention with a student and to check back to gauge progress toward intentions previously discussed (along with the class goal from the Crafting Session). The more we involve students in that process, the more likely they are to be engaged in realizing their intentions. They should be actively involved in the conference at every level: they share their work as evidence of growth toward intentions, they record questions to ask the teacher (or a peer) during conferences, they keep track of their progress in between conferences, and they create new goals and intentions alongside the teacher when appropriate. (See Appendix 2 for examples of students' record-keeping forms.) As the school year progresses, my hope is that students will gradually become more aware of their intentions and that they'll tell us what they strive to do as readers and writers. Help children avoid quantity-related goals, e.g. reading or writing more pages, longer and faster.

Another word or two about goals and intentions: The first thing to remember is that there is no one "right" goal for a child. At the beginning of the year, you'll review their early work and any meaningful assessment data and take the lead in developing individual goals in conferences, but very soon we need to expect students to monitor their learning, gauge how they have progressed, and to enter each conference with a stance that says, "Here's what I want to try next!" Our lead questions are always "What do you want to learn as a reader and a writer?" and "How can I help you do that?"

Although each child will be working toward the class goal (based on instruction from the Crafting Sessions), each should have at least one individual intention as well. It's ideal if their intention applies to both reading and writing, but if it doesn't, you'll make sure that the next intention focuses on the other area.

There are any number of productive directions you might choose depending on the child's energy and interest. I try as often as possible to suggest at least two goals, either of which will be helpful for the student, and invite them to choose which goal they would most like to work toward—I've learned not to be surprised when they tell me they want to try both! You may want to keep notes about the different options you have in mind so that you can suggest the unchosen goal later if they haven't already tackled it.

I occasionally interrupt the rest of the class (a check-in) after a conference to point out a success one child has experienced. Soon other children try the tactic I pointed out to the class.

> *We need to expect students to monitor their learning, gauge how they have progressed, and to enter each conference with a stance that says, "Here's what I want to try next!" Our lead questions are always "What do you want to learn as a reader and a writer?" and "How can I help you do that?"*

How Do We Know What Content to Teach in a Conference?

This might be a great time to take another look online at Thinking Strategies and Writer's Tools to review the strategies and tools. Although the list is not a compendium of everything that is important to teach, you will find many of the key concepts students must know and be able to use to progress as readers and writers. Of course, your state standards should be used as a resource, but most important are your observations about what students are already doing successfully and careful consideration about what new goals/intentions might be a logical next step for a given child. Your judgment, particularly if you confer regularly with students, is your true north. Once you know your kids as readers and writers, several new goals will be apparent.

This is how I think about goals and intentions. Some will be surface level (word learning and conventions) and some will be deep structure (creating meaning) levels.

SURFACE-LEVEL GOALS—THE VISIBLE AND AUDIBLE ASPECTS OF LANGUAGE

- After listening to a child read, focus on *one goal (or intention if the student suggests it)* that will help them identify words more consistently and read more fluently. For example, how readers and writers use punctuation to show pauses. Be certain that the child has a text in which they can practice that is about 85 to 90 percent decodable or one the child has heard read aloud multiple times. Talk about how the writer of their text has made meaning using tools like medial and ending punctuation. Think with the child about how they can use the goal in their writing as well as reading. Use your state's standards as a guide but be careful not to expand your focus to too many goals. It is fine to ask the child to apply previously taught targets along with a new goal, though.

- Review a child's writing and focus on *one goal or intention (if the student suggests it)* that will help them write in a more understandable and readable way. For example, think with your student about why and how authors use paragraphs. This is likely something that would have been taught in a Crafting Session, and you'll find yourself checking for application in a conference. Make certain that the child has a piece of writing they are excited about to apply the new goal. Ensure that the child has mentor texts they can use to refer to the ways other authors use the strategy or tool. Think with the child about how their goal as a writer is evidenced in text they are reading. Discuss ways that they, as readers, rely upon the strategy or tool to make meaning as they read.

DEEP STRUCTURE GOALS —THE INVISIBLE AND INAUDIBLE ASPECTS OF LANGUAGE

- Talk with the child about their understanding of the text they're reading or the piece they are writing. For example, students need to consider purpose and audience for their reading and writing. Explore several potential audiences for their writing, and make a plan for how they want to share their insights from reading with other readers. Help the child avoid retelling the text (or their writing focus) from beginning to end. Focus instead on what they think is most important to *know, feel, and believe* about the text they are reading and what they want readers of their writing to *know, feel, and believe* as they read it.

- Invite the student to use thinking strategies to make meaning clearer, whether they are reading or writing. (See the online resources for a complete list of reading and writing thinking strategies and writer's tools.) For example, you may have an overarching goal such as using images to understand text and write with more detail as a class, but if a child is struggling to decide what's most important in the text they are reading or if the child is trying to write in a way that will encourage their readers to infer, you can teach or review either of those strategies in a conference based on the child's need.

- Think with the child about what they are doing well as a reader and writer. For example, "You seem like the kind of reader who really notices how characters change. What does that suggest to you as a writer? What would you like to try next? Now that you've noticed how characters change, let's talk about internal change and external change. What have you noticed in the book you're reading? How can you try that goal as a reader? As a writer?"

We have long known that conferring provides us with great opportunities to differentiate for individual students, respond to their social and emotional needs, and ensure their progress toward academic goals. Conferences offer a space in which children can discuss their developing identities as readers and writers. I mentioned earlier that it is not within the scope of this book to explore every facet of conferring. Fortunately, Carl Anderson (2000, 2018) and Patrick Allen (2009) have written comprehensive guides to writing and reading conferences, respectively. Don't forget to check out some record-keeping ideas in Appendix 2. Feel free to amend them for your needs.

Sometimes nonexamples are helpful when explaining a new concept to kids; the same is true for us, so in Figure 7.1 I share some of the hard lessons I've learned over the years—a compendium of what *not* to do in conferences.

What to Avoid in Conferences

Conferring about the book or written piece only. A conference should also focus on how the reader or writer is creating meaning, how they are improving, what their intentions are. A conference isn't a chat about a book—it's an opportunity to assess and teach. Avoid having a chat about the book or written piece, rather than teaching to a specific goal or focusing on new learning for the reader/writer.

Focusing on more than one or two current goals. Just because you observe more challenges, don't think you need to tackle it all in one conference.

Asking the child to recall or retell unless you need a quick synthesis because you haven't read the book or the writing. Very few of these types of summaries will be necessary if we're conferring about thinking strategies and writer's tools. Discussion around a strategy such as how a reader infers and/or how a writer leaves information for their writer to infer will reveal how much the child knows about the text *and* help the child become more strategic.

Asking the child to read aloud unless you're assessing surface-structure systems.

Failing to give full attention to the child due to concerns about other children's behaviors. Get through the present conference before dealing with any disruptive behaviors. Avoid interruptions for any reason from other children.

Taking ownership from the child by taking the book or writing from their hands during the conference.

Taking ownership from the child by setting all the goals.

Creating other work options (centers, worksheets) for other students while you're conferring or meeting with a group. The rest of the class should be reading and/or writing with a focus on their goals.

Figure 7.1 What to Avoid in Conferences

Invitational Groups—Not Your Mother's Small-Group Instruction

It's late October and finally, finally the first graders in Jenn's classroom can sustain independent reading and writing during Composing for thirty minutes. She usually breaks Composing into two blocks with a check-in or two built in when things start to feel a little ragged. It feels like it has been a year, but looking around at these industrious little people, Jenn feels a sense of relief, gratitude, and amazement. They're six, *six*, and they can do this! She has time to confer with individuals and buddy-reading pairs. They are immersed in an informational text unit and using questioning and determining importance to integrate reading and writing.

We're still working on issues like balancing conferring and Invitational Groups.

—Fabviola Rosales, fifth-grade teacher, Milagro Elementary School,
   Los Angeles, CA

Recently, Jenn had noticed, as she poured through her conference notes (see Appendix 2 for her conference record-keeping form) that she had at least five children who hadn't generated the questions that she hoped would lead to some focus for their research project on animals of the world. In Crafting, Jenn modeled her own questions about bonobos in the Democratic Republic of Congo using the wonderful Martin Jenkins book *Ape*. She is fascinated by bonobos and hoped that her genuine interest in these primates would help her students see that our questions, when reading and writing informational text, guide us into deeper and more focused learning. Her goal was for children to generate many questions about animals of the world that fascinate them. She is getting ready to ask the students to use a sticky note pyramid to prioritize their questions—each child needed roughly three top priority questions. She planned to place the children in groups of three based on the similarity of their questions, for researcher's workshop. Together, they would explore texts and eventually publish their research.

Through Literacy Studio, students also get more of what they need . . . opportunities to engage in meaningful thinking, opportunities to regularly make authentic and meaningful choices as a reader and a writer, opportunities for regular, targeted feedback and intentional instruction, and opportunities to have reflective dialogue with and learn from peers. All of these are real, targeted, and worthy of students' time, which leads to significant increases in engagement. Student growth from this engagement is observable (visible, audible) from conference to conference, from notebook entry to notebook entry, from peer conference to peer conference, and from whole-class Crafting to Reflection.

—Erica Wood, Instructional Coach, Fire Prairie Upper Elementary,
  Fort Osage, MO

But at least five hadn't generated a single question. It's interesting to note that these five kiddos were very different readers and writers; some were very engaged and advancing well; others were striving. They weren't the same "level" but they shared a need—no questions!

It was a Tuesday morning; I was lucky enough to be in the room. Jenn, her first-grade colleagues, and I had just come from a planning session in which we decided to colead the first Invitational Group of the year in her classroom. The other teachers planned to observe, and we would put our heads together about how things went over lunch.

Jenn asked me to convene the Invitational Group—the kids had never seen one—and she wanted all her students to be part of the process, though only five were part of the group. It was so smart to think of it that way because we needed the students who wouldn't be part of the group to continue their work as readers and writers so that, uninterrupted, we could conduct the Invitational Group.

Following a Crafting Session in which Jenn modeled how to create a pyramid with questions on sticky notes to prioritize questions for study, I asked for the children's attention.

> **Me:** Good morning, ladies and gentlemen of the first grade. You're about to hear us invite five students to join us for some in-depth study on asking questions.

Not surprisingly, hands shot up.

Various students: I'll come! I want to come!

Me: I'm so glad you want to be part of the Invitational Group (written on an anchor chart) because before long, all of you will be invited. Today, though, I want to invite the following researchers.

I named the five students about whom Jenn was concerned.

Me: You need to know *why* I'm inviting those five children. Let me explain.

I named the children again.

Me: In our Invitational Group today, we'll be exploring where questions are born! Where do questions come from? How do readers and writers and researchers get questions? I want these five students to join me for a discussion about questions!

There was plenty of groaning, some yessss-ing, and some whys, but we got through that quickly.

Jenn and I sent the rest of the children off to read and write and kept the five with us. We walked around the room as a group of seven and I narrated, rather loudly, what the kids were doing to settle into their reading and writing. Some children had started to write their questions on sticky notes to create a pyramid, and we pointed that out: "Wow, that didn't take long!" After everyone had settled in, we pulled the newly formed Invitational Group to a small table. I often conduct Invitationals on the floor; either works.

Me: Welcome to our first Invitational Group. You five are the first to be invited. Congratulations!

They looked confused of course, but all would become clear soon enough. We wanted to be sure that they understood that being "invited" to a group was lucky, not something that they had to endure because they weren't getting it. We knew, of course, that this group shared a need, but we want them to see Invitational Groups as something of an honor.

Jenn: We want to thank you for joining us and tell you why we're here today. We've been talking about how questions, the things we wonder about in the world, can help us study new things as researchers.

I handed three pink unlined three-by-five-inch index cards to each child. Jenn had, brilliantly in my view, suggested that we offer them a larger, unlined surface to write on rather than the sticky notes on which many of the others were capturing questions. Perhaps the larger size would free them to write their questions.

Me: You are the first ones in this whole school year in this whole class to get to record your questions on index cards! Congratulations!

They looked at me with a bit of skepticism, but I wouldn't be deterred.

Me: We're going to talk today about how to get questions when you don't feel like you have any. Has that ever happened to any of you?

Nods all around.

Jenn: Me too, and it really helps me to have some colorful index cards to help me keep track of my questions.

At this point, I surreptitiously looked around the classroom. More than half were totally tuned in to our group. That doesn't matter; in fact, it may be great—they'll learn more about how Invitational Groups work, at least in these early days. I was determined not to let anything happening around us get us off course. If some children had a difficult time focusing after paying attention to our group for a while, we'll take it up later, but I will not let anything short of spurting blood from an artery draw our attention away from our group members.

Me: Let me show you these cards with my questions.

I read three questions I had written earlier. Two were phrased as "I wonder" statements and one was written as a question. All related to Jenn's (and my) interest in bonobos.

Almost immediately, Davey, one of the five, spoke up.

Davey: That one's not a question. It's an I wonder.

Aha! Interesting insight into a reason why he might be stuck. I assured him that I wonder statements were as acceptable as questions and he looked relieved, but still skeptical.

Me: Davey, do you have any I wonder statements about animals?

Davey: Yeah, I do. I told them (an apparent reference to the rest of the class) that I wonder about how bonobos are different than people.

I stopped myself from saying, "It's fairly obvious, right, dude?"

Jenn: Oh, Davey, you're remembering that bonobos are the most like humans of any of the large primates, aren't you?

Davey: Yep, but it's not a question.

Jenn tried again to reassure him that although she had recorded questions as she modeled, I wonder statements were just fine. He really was hanging on to that misconception.

Jenn: Really, Davey, I love I wonder statements. You can come up with as many as you want!

Finally, he seemed to accept it, but I had a hunch that this wasn't the only thing that was standing in Davey's way as he sought to generate questions.

Me: Davey, do you think you might have some I wonder statements about the animals you're curious about?

Davey: Yeah, I've got giraffes and dogs, and elephants and . . .

That list was going to go on for a while! I interrupted him.

Me: Oh my gosh, Davey. You can get started writing I wonders right now. You can head back to your writing space and capture all the things you wonder about animals on a card!

Jenn handed him more three-by-five-inch cards.

Jenn: Davey, one question or I wonder statement on each card, OK?

Off he went.

I have to interject here that when we come across a simple solution like this it seems silly to ask the child to continue in the group. He's ready to do the most important thing, read and write. There's no time like the present!

We turned back to the remaining four members of the Invitational Group and asked if any of them had questions or things they wondered about. Nope! Not a one . . .

Me: OK, you researchers, let me show you how I get my questions and wonders and then we can try it right here for you.

I pulled out several books including *Ape* that Jenn had *already read* to the class and thumbed through them, musing over pictures, generating some questions and wonders along the way. Invitational Groups are often just the additional opportunity kids need for some focused think-alouds and modeling.

It wasn't long before Alicia had a question. It happened to be exactly what I asked, but that's OK. She was trying to work out, in her mind, what it meant to have a question or wondering. These are very abstract concepts, and they're six! I was thrilled that we had even two out of the group who seemed to be catching some wind beneath their wings. We continued to think aloud and modeled writing our questions on index cards for another few minutes.

Me: OK, your turn! We'll turn the pages of this book without reading it, and you stop us when you wonder something or have a question.

That did the trick for two of them, including Alicia. The other two hadn't connected yet. We agreed to meet again in two days' time to see if they have questions and I wonder statements written on their index cards. I didn't want the Invitational Group to go on for too long—it's tough for the other kids to focus for long when we're not in circulation and I can't expect everyone in the group to get the concept on the first meeting. Invitational Groups often meet three times before everyone has addressed the need that brought them there in the first place. We stood up to adjourn.

Alex: Can we draw?

Jenn stopped them all.

Jenn: Wow, you guys, Alex just asked a great question. He wondered if you could share your question in a drawing. I think that's a great idea *and* I want you to try to put words along with your drawing so that when I come to confer with you, you'll be able to remember what your questions are. Does that sound fair?

Alex perked up immediately and hustled to his spot on the floor. We noticed that he began to draw immediately.

This little Invitational Group was just one in which I've been privileged to participate in recent years but it was one that drove home that power of convening kids with a shared need to focus, in just a bit more depth, on what we're asking them to do. Read on for the nitty-gritty about Invitational Groups for your children.

Remember earlier in the chapter where I mentioned that Literacy Studio is all about differentiation? We are fortunate to teach in an era where we can rethink small-group instruction in reading and writing—Invitational Groups comprise, in my view, the next horizon in small-group instruction and are a time-efficient way to differentiate. We know that small groups can be a hive of engagement and learning, but in our current conceptualization of small-group instruction, we find ourselves bogged down in an endless rotation of one small group after another, unsure of whether we're really making a difference for students.

In reading, we have been encouraged (Fountas and Pinnell 2012/2013) to move away from small-group instruction in which small groups are convened based on a child's reading "level." We understand that an assessed reading level can give us only a narrow glimpse of all the factors that influence readability for an individual child. We know that we need to convene students who have *shared needs*, *not levels*, as readers. And think about small groups in writing. What? Is there such a thing? We rarely take the opportunity to gather small groups of writing for instruction. Why wouldn't we convene a group of writers who share a goal or have similar intentions?

In a Literacy Studio, we conceive of small-group teaching and learning in an entirely different way. We *invite* (though in fairness, there will be no RSVPing "no") children to join us because, through observations and conferences, we have become aware that they share a particular need and/or they are ready to explore new vistas in their language use. They are invited to gather for two or more small-group meetings, of about ten minutes, not because they have been assessed at the same reading level or because they are reading the same book but because they have demonstrated in their actual reading and/or writing that they will benefit from additional or new, sometimes more advanced, instruction. They share a need.

In Literacy Studio, we are not plodding through three small reading groups each day (which robs us of time to confer and stigmatizes students) with the same children, taking turns, reading aloud, often in a round-robin fashion. Instead, there will be many days where the teacher does not host an Invitational Group at all and confers throughout the Composing Session. But that doesn't make sense if there is an evident pattern of need to confer with four or five (but it could be three or seven!) different students who share that need. The teacher may convene the group to meet two, three, or more times to focus on a particular goal and check progress on the focus of the Invitational Group instruction, but eventually the group will disband and new groups will form, again, because they share a need. Invitational Groups are dynamic, engaging, focused, and *impermanent*.

Let's recap a bit about Invitational Groups, and investigate characteristics of effective Invitational Groups, and, importantly, explore what Invitational Groups are *not*.

A Deeper Dive into Invitational Groups

Invitational groups are *short* (no more than ten minutes), focused, and active. They usually don't meet more than once or twice each week and rarely more than three times total as a group focused on a particular concept or intention. The group's members are only together because, through conferences and observation, their teacher has identified a common need among them. An Invitational Group might include readers or writers who are very advanced alongside striving readers and writers because they share a need.

I may use a more accessible text than those I used in Crafting Sessions on the same topic, and I rarely read a whole text I'm using for instruction. Invitational Groups are primarily focused on giving kids a chance to experiment with or reinforce concepts recently taught but that they have not yet applied. I love to engage the kids in writing very short pieces, what I call "try its" in Invitational Groups; it gives me a chance to observe, assess, and provide feedback in the moment. If I'm focused on reading, I try to make the connections to writing explicit and vice versa.

I'm still working on being more flexible with my planning to ensure that we can continue to practice into the Literacy Studio and get to a point where we can't remember it ever being anything different!

—Karla Contreras, second-grade teacher, Milagro Elementary School,
   Los Angeles, CA

The same instructional tools we use in Crafting (thinking aloud, modeling, and demonstrating, see Chapters 4 and 5) apply in Invitational Groups, but in an Invitational Group, I want to review the concept much more quickly, give the group members time to experiment with it right then and there, and then adjourn. I like to look at Invitational Groups as an opportunity for more intensive instruction, but also as a time to experiment, with the support of others, with class goals and student intentions. Children are actively and enthusiastically involved, and the group generates a spirit of support for other group members. Often, I conclude an Invitational Group by brainstorming with the members about how we can share or "teach" others what we've tried to do in an upcoming Reflecting Session (see Chapter 8). They leave with a goal and know that they will be expected to apply the concept in their reading and writing before the next Invitational Group. Groups usually do not meet on consecutive days; they need time in Composing to apply what they have discussed in an Invitational Group before they reconvene with their group.

Too often we struggle to find ways to accelerate learning for students who are ready. Invitational Groups are also for challenging some of our most advanced language users to try something the rest of the class may not be ready to try. Let's contrast Invitational Groups with other types of small-group instruction with which you may be familar.

INVITATIONAL GROUPS VS. OTHER TYPES OF SMALL-GROUP LITERACY LEARNING

- Invitational Groups are not static—the same group of children may meet one to three times to focus on an area of need, usually identified through conferences.

- Invitational Groups are not convened because the children have the same assessed reading or writing "level."

- Invitational Groups are not homogeneous in terms of the complexity of the text they are reading or the sophistication of their writing—they exhibit a similar need in whatever they are reading and writing.

- Invitational Groups are designed to offer instruction in the groups' zone of proximal development—in other words, instruction stretches students to the next level based on a clearly identified need for each child in the group.

- Invitational Groups are not used as an opportunity for the teacher to listen to children read aloud in a round-robin style or each read their writing aloud.

- When the teacher is working with an Invitational Group, the other children are reading and writing.

- When the teacher is working with an Invitational Group, they do not permit interruptions from other students, nor do they initiate the interruption to manage other children.

- The teacher creates a sense of anticipation and excitement for those invited to a group and may open the group to others who believe they share the same need.

- Children who have participated in an Invitational Group are often invited to teach or demonstrate to others what they have learned during Crafting or Reflecting times.

Back to Where We Started: It's All About Differentiating!

Why approach small-group and individual instruction this way? Because when we know better, we do better. We understand that, to the degree possible, it's essential to understand each student's needs and to differentiate our instruction. If we want engaged students who are learning to love reading and writing, we need to ensure that we tailor our responses as much as possible for them, which means conferences and some small groups.

In Chapter 8, we'll investigate several ways that students solidify new learning through global questions, teaching others, and reflecting on how they have changed and grown as readers and writers.

CHAPTER EIGHT

Reflection

The Home for Important Questions and Life Lessons

Referring to children, Pablo Casals, internationally known cellist and humanitarian, said, "We should say to each of them 'Do you know what you are? You are a marvel. You are unique. You have the capacity for anything. Yes, you are a marvel. And when you grow up, can you then harm another who is, like you, a marvel? You must cherish one another. You must work—we all must work—to make this world worthy of its children.'" How grateful I am to have Casals' words to lead a chapter on Reflection.

Before Literacy Studio

Time: 11:45

Place: Your classroom

Activity: Writer's workshop

Time is tight. You need to have the students in the cafeteria in ten minutes. They're writing. You glance at the clock. Decision time. Do you let the students continue what is obviously a productive independent work time or do you gather them to share? You glance around and see that a couple of students who haven't focused on writing nearly enough in the month since school started are actually (finally) writing. That's it. No sharing time today. Again. Let them keep writing.

Honestly, it's the decision I would make; if they're writing well, let them keep going. Before Literacy Studio, we often found that after two minilessons, two workshop times, four transitions, there really wasn't time to give students a chance to reflect on their learning and connect it to the world outside the classroom. Sharing time often felt limp and unengaging, just a stream of kids wanting to share what they worked on that day with very little deference to what other readers and writers were learning and with few meaty conversations for everyone to, well, reflect on.

Many teachers with whom I work are frustrated by sharing time, what we'll call Reflection in Literacy Studio. Does this sound familiar? "OK, Joachim, thanks for sharing. Any comments or questions? No? OK, who wants to share next? Angelina, you want to share what you've been reading? Well, we're sharing writing today, you'll have to wait until tomorrow." The next day (or more likely three days later because you ran out of time for sharing), Angelina climbs into the sharing chair, reads aloud from a book she loves. She, too, is allowed to take one question and one comment and then is asked to choose another child to share; the latter process takes longer than the sharing and comments combined. It is coma inducing. I'm sorry, but really, when a child is merely "sharing," what is everyone else learning?

Let me qualify that point a bit: we want kids to share and interact with each other about the books they read and the writing they're doing; sharing is important for oral language development, for developing confidence and a sense of audience for writers, for discussing ideas in texts for readers, for recommending books, and for getting excited about what's next. I am concerned, however, that we are still employing some rather tired approaches in the sharing component of our literacy work. Children do share in a Literacy Studio Reflection Session (and more informally during Crafting and Composing), but it doesn't start and end there. We need to consider ways to boost engagement during Crafting and Composing so that children have something worth sharing. The point of Reflection Sessions in the Literacy Studio, however, is to spark true reflection for the child who is sharing and to inform the others who are not.

Reflection is not simply sharing time. We can inject much more energy, engagement, and learning into this essential component of the Literacy Studio. It's going to become tougher to say "Oh well, no sharing today" after you read this chapter. I hope.

How do we transform sharing time into true Reflection? Let's start with an overview of Reflection as I envision it in the Literacy Studio. Then we'll explore the connecting role of global questions, how we can invite students to "teach" each other or share an excerpt, followed by some final words about how to inject new life into sharing our reading and writing, to keep things spicy!

> The change to a Literacy Studio model has created a beautiful, dynamic, powerful learning time and space in which my students see themselves as designers, creators, and mentors. Our sense of what matters is constantly growing and evolving. Overall, their engagement, ownership, and transfer of skills have improved.
>
> —Modesta Urbina, third-grade teacher, Milagro Elementary School, Los Angeles, CA

What Is a Reflection Session?

Reflection is a time for the class to think together about teacher- or student-generated global questions and to share progress as readers and writers. Reflection is student centered, student led whenever possible. I love to have the children gathered on the floor in a circle or oval rather than in a group as they are for most Crafting Sessions, so that they can see each other. Usually, Reflection lasts about ten minutes and often comes at the end of the Literacy

Studio, but remember the planning wheel: we can enter Literacy Studio with Crafting, Composing, or Reflection; once the children are accustomed to Literacy Studio, it's great to change the entry point—keep them guessing! We can start the Studio with Reflecting or inject Reflection into the middle of the Composing time, rather like a longer check-in. It's important to remember that Composing Sessions take precedence; if we spend more time in Reflection, we may need to cut back on Crafting to leave students with enough time to read and write.

Reflection is a time to discuss texts students love and each other's writing. I love the lively conversations that emanate from a provocative book or student writing. In Reflection, students share what they have learned or tried with other readers and writers. But Reflecting is more than sharing; we can take it to the next level. For example, I learned, from observing in British classrooms, that Reflection can be an opportunity for readers and writers to *teach* others about their use of a certain tool or strategy. You know how clearly we understand a concept when we teach it; the same is true for students. When a child prepares to *teach* a concept that they've applied in their own writing or reading, the concept becomes more concrete in their long-term memory, making their learning last longer and become applicable to future learning situations.

The teacher's role in Reflecting includes demonstrating various ways in which readers and writers can share and respond to each other, helping children to make connections between reading and writing, but then standing back to let students lead the conversation as much as possible. Reflection can be especially powerful if you invite a child or two to share something they tried from which the whole group would benefit. When you're conferring or hosting Invitational Groups, keep your eye out for concepts children are trying—it doesn't have to be "mastered." After the invited child shares, it's very helpful for others to weigh in on how they have or may try the same tool or strategy.

The Teacher's Role in Reflecting

Let's take a closer look at the teacher's role in Reflecting. Our role lies in modeling how to listen and respond appropriately. For example, in responding to a child who is sharing their work, the teacher might model and then expect the listeners to

- listen and demonstrate how to respond appropriately
- recognize and name the child's insight or demonstrated new learning
- connect responses about what has been read to the children's writing and vice versa
- ask questions to deepen the students' understanding of a text or piece of student writing
- ask questions about their peer's process, plans, and ideas about how something they have tried will be useful to other readers/writers
- propose new strategies or tools, ways to continue the work
- challenge what is being shared to push the student and others to expand their thinking.

The Student's Role in Reflecting

Let's take a quick peek at what matters most in Reflection. These simple principles can help us revitalize this very important component of the Literacy Studio.

- Students use global questions (see below) to link their learning to big ideas and issues outside the classroom and to learning they are and have been doing across the curriculum, throughout the year.

- They share their excitement about particular texts and their writing, but in a way that encourages others as readers and writers.

- They reflect on their own learning, talk about how they have grown as readers and writers, regain engagement and momentum, and set new goals.

- They are never compelled to share, but we encourage them to do so in the most comfortable structure for them—whole group, small group, trios, or pairs. We gently and gradually encourage reluctant children to share with larger groups by focusing on how worthy their thinking is and how the rest of the class deserves to learn from them.

- They use a wide variety of ways to share their progress as readers and writers—they focus not on retelling or summarizing a book, nor merely reading their writing aloud, but on discussing their *thinking* about a text and sharing their ideas, intentions, and struggles as a writer in a way that might be helpful to other readers and writers.

- They teach others what they have attempted as readers and writers. These sessions can be in pairs, trios, small or large groups. Students may prepare a lesson and consider ways to teach in a way that all learners' needs will be met.

Global Questions

I come from an inquisitive family. My ninety-one-year-old father who passed away as I was writing this chapter in August 2021, was question asker in chief. Before the pandemic we had lunch together every week, probably since before most readers of this book were born. Those lunches were his venue for asking me questions. Where was I traveling in the coming week? What was the school district like? What was my focus going to be with my clients? What flying stories did I have from last week? What did I think about the new secretary of education? Why wasn't I the secretary of education (I know,

I know, but he's my *dad!*)? How might education funding be improved? Why didn't I believe in test scores as the best metric for success in public schooling? He barely drew breath. He always asked those questions; I've grown accustomed to them and am now an inquisitor with my daughter and nephew.

All those questions, therefore, made for an uneasy settling into the role of teacher for me. When I started teaching, it was all about the answers. The questions I was instructed to ask were of a distinctly convergent variety. Get the answers down, grade the papers, enter the scores into the little, tiny squares in the grade book. I was unhappy, but so keen (get it?) to do the right thing, to do what it took to be a teacher, to fit in. I tried to find joy in the task-completion mentality that drove teaching and learning in my first school, but it wasn't very joyful. I guess part of me just assumed that this was the reality in education and the price I had to pay for spending my days with children.

The bright spot came every day when I ate lunch with my students and found that the brief time when they inhaled their peanut butter and jelly sandwiches was prime time for questions. Sitting on the uncomfortable cafeteria bench, I could ask as many as I wanted; I could get to know them; I could learn about their lives, what drove them, what burdens they carried. It was joyful, it was poignant, it provided innumerable insights. And then we went back to the classroom. And plodded along. And turned in papers. And graded. And filled in the tiny squares. And repeated. My dad would have been quite disappointed.

Today, we understand the power of inquiry in teaching and learning. We know about researcher's workshop from wonderful resources like *Inquiry Illuminated: Researcher's Workshop Across the Curriculum* (Goudvis, Harvey, and Buhrow 2019). We know how a great question or two can launch hours, days, even months of engaged learning. We understand that children's questions are often far more engaging than our own, and, importantly, we know that questions aren't interrogatives waiting for an answer; they are food for thought. They are meant to be pondered, revisited, discussed, written about, and they are generative—great questions lead to new questions. And, to my point in this chapter, questions lead to reflection.

I believe we can boost engagement and link concepts throughout a unit with what I'll call *global questions*—questions that extend the reach of student learning beyond the four walls of the classroom, questions that are posed, discussed, written about, revisited, and explored in Reflection.

Global questions are akin to what authors Jay McTighe and Grant Wiggins have called essential questions, but with a few key differences. According to McTighe and Wiggins, there are seven defining characteristics of an essential question.

A good essential question

1. Is *open-ended*; that is, it typically will not have a single, final, and correct answer.

2. Is *thought-provoking* and *intellectually engaging*, often sparking discussion and debate.

3. Calls for *higher-order thinking*, such as analysis, inference, evaluation, prediction. It cannot be effectively answered by recall alone.

4. Points toward *important, transferable ideas* within (and sometimes across) disciplines.

5. Raises *additional questions* and sparks further inquiry.

6. Requires *support* and *justification*, not just an answer.

7. *Recurs* over time; that is, the question can and should be revisited again and again. (McTighe and Wiggins 2013, 3)

Global questions rest on the foundation of essential questions—all the characteristics listed above are true for global questions, but global questions are also based on these key ideas.

1. Global questions are anchors, a through line, for daily discussions in all components of the Literacy Studio.

2. Global questions connect students' learning to social justice and equity issues.

3. Global questions are frequently student generated and can lead to inquiry work for individuals or groups.

4. Global questions help students connect to the world outside the classroom, including topics related to other disciplines.

5. Global questions provide an opportunity to connect back to learning throughout the year and across the curriculum.

6. Global questions provide the focus for Reflection.

In a Literacy Studio, Reflection, the time when students share texts and writing, their successes and struggles, and reflect on their growth as language users, is anchored in global questions. Let's talk about a few global questions I've used in my work with schools and districts around the country. As you read through Figure 8.1, please keep these notes of caution in mind:

1. Some of the questions may seem abstract or too "high level" for the grade levels I've listed. I've found that even young children can and want to discuss complex topics and that doing so helps them engage in and shape their developing belief systems. I cannot recall a single time where, with proper scaffolding, students haven't been able to really dig into a lofty global question. Of course, you and your students will shape your own global questions, but don't underestimate what your children can and should discuss.

2. These questions don't exist in a vacuum. They are anchors for units of study in some examples and, when not embedded in a literacy unit, can stem from topics and discussions in science, social studies, art, and beyond. The fifth-grade sample global question in Figure 8.1 is part of a genre study.

3. Global questions emerge spontaneously from class discussion in some cases; sometimes they are designed by the teacher and refined through discussion. There is no "right" way to develop a global question. I like to use *how*, *why*, or *in what ways* as a start.

4. There are often several global questions in play (and posted prominently around the room) for a given unit or period of time. It's common for a class to discuss a global question for

A Sampling of Global Questions	
Context	**Global Question(s)**
Kindergarten Launching the year's work in conjunction with building community in the classroom	How do people share emotions with others? When is it important to share emotions? What are all the ways we can use language to share emotions? How and why do we share emotions in our classroom?
First grade Exploratory study using texts that explore equity and writing to persuade	What is fair? How do we know if something is fair or unfair? How do others' ideas about what is fair differ from our own? Why is it important to think about what is fair?
Second grade Unit focused on asking questions in nonfiction texts and on embedding questions directly into students' own nonfiction writing	In what ways do people use questions to help them understand the social and natural world? How can we use questions to address conflict?
Third grade Synthesis unit focused on how we change our thinking and actions because of books and how we seek to change our audience's thinking as we write	How do books (and other media) and our writing lead to changes in our thinking, our emotions, our beliefs, and our actions in the world?
Fourth grade Student-led inquiry in which students decided to explore how a wide range of fictional characters, historical characters, and people they have known have addressed and grown from challenges	In what ways do challenges in life shape our interactions with other people, particularly those whose lived experiences are different from our own?
Fifth grade Genre unit focused on persuasive writing	In what ways has persuasive writing and speech been used to provoke and respond to social change? How can you use persuasive writing to provoke and/or respond to social change?

* Please note: These samples were developed as part of other teachers' work and are therefore unlikely to be applicable in your classroom.

Figure 8.1 A Sampling of Global Questions

several weeks, sometimes longer. The goal is not to answer the question(s), but to generate new thinking and new questions, to solidify learning, and, in some cases, affirm or challenge students' beliefs.

5. Global questions can be the starting point for individual and group inquiry. Great questions are generative, as I've said— they lead to other questions. Follow where they lead!

Let's drop in on a Reflection Session that sprung from a global question. In fact, it's the question listed under third grade in Figure 8.1: How do books (and other media) and our writing lead to changes in our thinking, our emotions, our beliefs, and our actions in the world?

The teacher, Rafael, had observed that many of his students formed opinions very early in the texts they read and didn't revise them with new thinking as they continued to read. In conferences, several students had shared their ideas about the gist of the texts they were reading as if they hadn't read beyond the first few pages. It seemed that they were holding on for dear life to the early concepts they understood and seemed to be inflexible in terms of changing their thinking.

In writing, he noticed a related problem. When writing narrative texts, some students described every move they made from the moment they crawled out of bed to the minute they lay their heads upon the pillow at night. Popularly known as the bed-to-bed story and quite common in the second- through fourth-grade age group, these coma-inducing narratives included descriptions in which children not only wrote about brushing their teeth but informed us of the kind of toothpaste they liked best!

To address these issues, he immersed his third graders in a unit that incorporated synthesis, a thinking strategy (see Thinking Strategies and Writer's Tools [available online]). In Crafting, the class had observed Rafael's think-alouds and had been engaged in talking about how their thinking changes as they read. Rafael had pulled an Invitational Group to focus on the bed-to-bed writing; it wasn't a problem with which the whole class was struggling.

To unite what would typically be separate strands for reading and writing, he designed the global question to be used in Crafting Sessions, conferences, and especially in Reflection. Of course, Rafael addressed these challenges in conferences and Invitational Groups, but for our purposes in this chapter, let's take a peek at his use of the global question in one Reflection session. It was inspiring!

Rafael gathered the third graders in the meeting area on a rug for Reflecting by ringing a series of chimes. Many students reluctantly put their books and writing away; others brought their pieces and texts with them to Reflecting. Instead of sitting in a group facing him, he configured them in an oval so they could see each other as they reflected. They knew (and had rehearsed many times) the procedure. I watched them make room for others in the circle, readjust their positions to see each other, and prepare to engage in conversation.

Rafael referred briefly to the global question posted on an anchor chart. Under the question, students had written their thoughts and responses, not only those that emerged during Reflection Sessions, but those that had struck them during Crafting and Composing as well. The anchor chart had become

a vessel for students' emerging thinking about how texts and other media cause people to change their thinking, emotions, and beliefs and actions. Most of the entries on the anchor chart related to changes students had experienced in their thinking while reading—many students had written about how the text they were reading had surprised them in some way. Rafael predicted that would happen following a Crafting Session in which he had thought aloud about how he was surprised as he read. So far, there were only a few student responses related to changes in their emotions or beliefs and only one related to a child's writing. The anchor chart had become an assessment tool for Rafael; he had only to look at the types of responses captured so far to know where they needed to go next.

> **Rafael:** I'm curious to hear from a couple of you about what you're thinking as writers this morning. Our global question (How do books [and other media] and our writing lead to changes in our thinking, our emotions, our beliefs, and our actions in the world?) refers to changes in thinking, emotions, and beliefs we experience when we read, but I want to know how, as writers, you're manipulating your reader's thinking, emotions, and beliefs.

Silence.

> **Rafael:** OK, let's think about how your thinking changes as you read, and most importantly, why your thinking changes.

Several students nodded (the signal that they wanted to share—Rafael prefers nonverbal signals rather than hand raising in Reflection).

> **Rafael:** Grace, what have you noticed?"

> **Grace:** Well, authors surprise you and make you think something new.

> **Rafael:** So true, we've talked about that, haven't we? And Grace, tell me something about how authors do that.

> **Grace:** They put stuff in that surprises you.

It was a somewhat circular response. Rafael and I spoke later and decided to focus upcoming think-alouds on other ways authors cause readers to change their thinking.

> **Rafael:** OK, so let's talk about how you, as writers, can cause your readers to change their thinking.

The next responses were predictable; put something in your writing that surprises the reader. Rafael asked if any of them had tried to include something surprising in their writing; no one indicated that they had. While observing, I predicted that he would end the Reflection by saying that others should try to use surprise to change their readers' thinking, but Rafael was just silent for a moment and that turned out to make all the difference.

Araceli raised her hand.

Araceli: In my story about my grandpa, I don't want to surprise my readers.

Rafael: OK, Araceli, what kinds of thinking are you trying to change in your piece?

Araceli: I'm trying to make everyone as sad as I am.

Rafael: Why is that important to you?

Araceli: Because other kids might have had their grandpas die and they'll know why it's sad.

Rafael: Say more, Araceli.

Araceli: Well, sometimes it's, it helps.

Rafael: Hmm, so it helps . . .

Araceli: Yeah, because you're not the only one who lost your grandpa.

Rafael: Right, yeah.

Rafael was pulling way back. Just let her expand her thinking.

Araceli: Yeah, I want them to cry because I cried so much.

Eddie: It's like feelings. We talked about how you can make your reader have feelings.

Rafael: Umm, . . .

Rafael's response was very quiet.

Rafael: So, what are you saying here, everyone? Why would writers want their readers to feel sad, or feel anything, really?

Here a dozen or more students nodded vigorously indicating that they wanted to respond. And that's when Rafael withdrew (almost) completely.

Rafael: The Reflection is yours, Alyson.

He was handing the control of the session to the students.

Alyson: It's like you said before, if you feel something like what the author feels, it's like empathy!

Many head nods.

Alyson: Matt, would you like to share?

Matt: Yes, thank you, Alyson. Yeah empathy. It's when you feel what someone else feels and you can be like more understanding about them. Araceli, it's like your grandpa. Someone else whose grandpa died can understand.

Rafael: Can empathize. So why is it important in the world to empathize? I'm thinking here not just about readers and writers, but about people in their lives, every day.

Here, Rafael pivoted to the world outside the classroom, the realm of global questions. It was a very simple segue, just enough of a prompt to help the students move from their focus on their reading and writing to the bigger questions related to living in a compassionate way.

As he voiced the question, his voice trailed off and about thirty seconds of silence followed. This class has learned to use silence in their Reflections. They know the power of silence. They've talked about it; Rafael has modeled and valued it. Now they use it.

Finally, Janyha spoke.

Janyha: Is it that people will be nicer?

She wanted Rafael to say whether she was right or not. He merely raised his eyebrows.

Skye: It is that people will be nicer, but they will get that they aren't the only ones who have had bad stuff happen.

JaVon: And, yeah, if you know that someone has had bad stuff happen, it's like you can think about their life, not just yours.

Rafael: So why is that important?

JaVon: Because if you're thinking about other people, you're going to not think bad stuff about them and that means there won't be fights.

Rafael: Hmm, OK, you readers and writers, let's think about this tonight. You've said a couple important things. You said that one way to change thinking as a writer is to inject surprise into your story; you also said that it's important to think about how your reader is feeling and to try, as a

Modesta Urbina and Third-Grade Students

writer, to make them feel certain ways; you've said that one of those ways is to cause the reader to empathize with what the characters are feeling; and finally you said that empathy is important in the world beyond reading and writing because it leads to people understanding each other and having less conflict. Is that right? Turn to the person sitting on your right, one group of three, and tell that person what you think was important from your Reflection today.

As they headed off to lunch, I exchanged a glance with Rafael. Wow. To start out with "the author of the text surprised me" and to end up with "empathy can lead to diminished conflict in the world" was pretty great and there is no way he could have known where that conversation would head when he essentially withdrew from it. A couple of well-placed observations and questions from him and they were able to go from focal to global. This is why we use global questions.

Often, the teacher launches a school year with their global questions, but it is important to talk to students about what characterizes a global question and to incorporate their questions as early and often as possible. Sometimes a group of students in a book club, for example, will generate their own global questions to anchor their discussion. Students love to write possible responses to global questions following an energetic discussion. They often jump into writing believing that they have "the answer" and discover that a global question is meant to be pondered. They are designed to spark discussion in Reflection and beyond. They are the connective tissue that can make a Reflection so much more meaningful and the ideas shared there much more lasting.

Children as Teachers: A New Take on Reflection

As I mentioned earlier, we want students to have daily opportunities to share their thinking about books and their successes and struggles as writers. Sharing builds listening and speaking skills, obviously, but also helps students develop confidence as readers and writers and helps them understand that they have something worth sharing. Sharing also provides the impetus to keep going—as a student discusses their writing, new ideas pop into their mind and they become eager to test them out in their written pieces. If a student is struggling to maintain the momentum while reading a longer text, sharing and discussing it with others can help them reengage with the text.

So how do we avoid the kind of sharing that mostly benefits the child who is sharing? I've found that if I change the way I think about what it means to share, I can breathe new life into Reflection. Years ago, I was part of an initiative in which US educators visited schools in London—yes, the one in Great Britain—I know, tough duty, but someone had to do it! I was dazzled by dozens of observations in British classrooms—how the educators juggled large class sizes where there may be as many as ten languages spoken within the same class, and how, despite challenging conditions, these educators personalized and facilitated learning rather than directing it. So many of the British classrooms we visited represented the ideal of a child-centered classroom. Along the way, I picked up some wonderful ideas about how to facilitate students' sharing time. One idea made a particularly strong impression. If a child wants to share, teachers often invite them to teach their peers rather than just share. It's a subtle difference, but an important one. Teachers discover, often through conferences, when a child is ready to teach and, especially at the beginning of the school year, invite the children to teach following a conference. As the year goes on, students often initiate a "teaching session" because they know they have discovered something in their own reading and writing that could benefit others.

For example, if a child has been learning to build suspense in a piece of writing (see Thinking Strategies and Writer's Tools online), they may be invited to share a portion of a longer piece in which they tried it. The writer may share parts of mentor texts they studied to see how published writers build tension and suspense. Or they may have conferred with other writers and their teacher and learned how to build toward a suspenseful part slowly, leaving the reader to wonder and predict what's likely to happen; they may have worked to use specific language that evokes suspense; they may have used setting to build toward a frightening part; they may have injected a surprise event to rattle the reader. They share, they teach, the *ways* they approached the writing as well as a portion of the writing. As a result, any student who wants to try something similar has a road map.

As every teacher knows, there are few ways to learn something so deeply as to teach it. Asking students to teach their peers shows that everyone in the room is a learner *and* a teacher, that learning doesn't just come from the adult teacher. Teaching their peers requires a bit of preparation as well. The student sharing must organize their thinking, create a brief plan for teaching, think about how to capture the key points (on an anchor chart, for example), and, importantly, needs to imagine how they might invite their "students" to be active learners. Does the student sharing ask the others to turn and talk, for example? Do they invite a small group of students who would like to try to build tension and suspense in their writing to meet later as an Invitational Group to try it together? In other words, the student sharing must consider if other students are actually learning! They must plan what to say, how to keep the "lesson" short, and how to invite questions along the way. Sure, that child could read her writing aloud to the others, but how much more powerful is it to leave them with something they too can try as readers and writers?

I have found that student ownership and student-driven learning is much higher. Students seek feedback from each other and are more accepting of feedback because it aligns with what they cared enough to write about. Now they want to share their learning with others. Peer conversations became more authentic. Students became and sought out mentors independently.

—Fabviola Rosales, fifth-grade teacher, Milagro Elementary School, Los Angeles, CA

One morning early in the school year, a colleague and I were conferring in a first-grade classroom. We pulled up next to Sammy, who looked to be about three and a half or four—you know how young first graders look at the beginning of the year! Sammy appeared completely disinterested in talking about what she intended to try as a writer. She asked how to spell *retriever* as in *golden retriever* and appeared as if she was going to say, "Thanks for stopping by—see ya!" Her teacher asked if we might, as long as we were there, hear about what she was trying as a writer. She immediately started to read her writing aloud.

Me: Oh, Sammy, so sorry. You don't need to read it to us, honey. Just tell us what you're trying to do. What do you want your readers to think and feel when they read your writing?

Sammy: Just that I got a golden retriever puppy.

Me: Wow, that's pretty exciting. What do you want your readers to know about your puppy?

Sammy: Just how do you spell *retriever*?

Sammy was nothing if not focused!

Me: Let's see what you've tried.

Rtvre. The class had been talking about silent *e*'s at the end of some words. Most kids were adding a silent *e* to every word!

Me: OK, that's a great start, Sammy. What do you want your readers to know?

Sammy: His name is Rufus.

Rfs.

Right there it was in the text.

Me: When you're with Rufus, what happens and what do you feel?

Sammy: He just licks me all over and over and it's so funny and he drools all over and he bites, but he doesn't mean to, and he ate my brother's shoe but he didn't mean to and then my mom stepped on him but she didn't mean to and he made this noise . . .

It was the classic case of so much to say and so little on the paper.

Me: Well, Sammy, you have so much to say about Rufus. What means the most to you? What do you really want your readers to know?

Sammy: That he's soooo funny.

Me: How are you going to let them know?

Sammy: Here, I'll read it to you!

Me: That's OK, sweetie, what I care most about is that you take this time to use words and pictures to tell us how funny Rufus is.

Sammy: But I'm supposed to read it.

Me: You know, let me tell you a bit about how some writers work. It's really helpful to read it aloud sometimes; I read my writing aloud to myself all the time. And it's OK not to read your writing aloud every time you confer with a teacher. Sometimes it's more important to get the words down, and you have so much to say.

Sammy: Yeah, but I can't spell it.

It won't be difficult for early years teachers to imagine the conversation we had. You know the drill: it's important to get the ideas down, we'll circle back to spell the words that are most important to you after you draft it, let's make a list of the ideas you most want to include, how will you make sure your readers know what is so funny about Rufus . . .

At the end of the conference, I invited Sammy to teach the other children what she had learned about writer's priorities. She was still pretty obsessed with the correct spellings, but she agreed to wait until later to edit. The thing that struck her was that she didn't have to read her piece aloud every time a teacher conferred with her. We rehearsed what she might say and later in Reflection, she held the class spellbound.

> **Me:** Sammy, I think you have something you would like to teach today?

> **Sammy:** Yep. So. You know how when you have a conference and you read your writing out loud?

They knew.

> **Sammy:** And you know how you don't know how to write the words?

It was a bit less clear, but they still nodded in affirmation.

> **Sammy:** Well, just read it to yourself. Then you're going to know what to write next and you can read it out loud, just not too loud!

I almost hesitate in sharing this little story because the conferring moves are predictable; you would have done the same. What stayed with me after Sammy "taught," though, was how new it was to *her*. She was the one who had the epiphany, and, in the end, it was significant to her and to others. Read your work aloud to yourself and push forward even though you don't know how to spell all the words. Had the teacher already taught those two things? I'm guessing she had, but it's just that much more impactful when the teacher is a kid.

It seems hard to overstate the power of asking kids to articulate their learnings to others. Teaching in Reflection doesn't happen every day, of course. It is, however, an important lever we can pull to make Reflection more engaging and meaningful.

The Joy of Sharing

I probably don't even have to write about this form of Reflecting; it's fairly obvious, but just in case, I want to remind us that sharing text is a joyful, motivating exercise that knits a community of readers and writers ever closer. Think about how you mark portions in a book to share with your book club! Just to have the opportunity to read a beautiful or haunting or riveting excerpt aloud is an important way to make the memory of a book live on. And to receive feedback on one's writing is a simultaneously terrifying and exhilarating experience! When I submit a chapter to my beloved editor and dear friend, Tom Newkirk, I dread but live in eager anticipation until he has read it and shared his thoughts. It's an act of trust to share one's writing.

I've observed that teachers who create a classroom climate that emphasizes a mindset of revision—we are all constantly getting better as readers and writers; we embrace struggle and seek to challenge ourselves as readers and writers; we actually *enjoy* rereading and revising our writing; we expect to rethink our work based on feedback from others—are most often rewarded with children who are eager to share and who view revision as part of the joy of deepening their understanding of texts and coaxing their writing into a clearer, more meaningful state. Revision and Reflection work hand in hand. When a child is invited to share, it's the revision we want to hear about—how did they start the day as a reader and writer, and how are they different now?

Similarly, when the class is on the lookout for examples of beautiful language in a book and a more concise way to write, everyone is learning. Sharing the struggles and successes affirms kids' efforts. We want to make room for students to come to a sharing session and say, "I just love this book!" and read an excerpt. We want kids to share the third attempt to create tension and suspense in their writing and to say, "I think I've finally got it!"

In Figure 8.2, I share a few options as you consider how to structure Reflecting Sessions. Eventually, students will suggest their own structures for Reflection.

Let's promise each other that we won't forgo Reflection because it feels limp and tired—let's breathe new life into these sessions to give kids a chance to practice listening and speaking, concretize their learning, share their struggles and successes, and teach each other. You'll be surprised and delighted by the impact of global questions and students as teachers on Reflecting Sessions. The connections we can make through our use of global questions make it more likely that students will retain and reapply what they have learned. The spotlight global questions shine on social justice issues will lead to more in-depth writing and focused reading, and students will begin to understand how crucial their voices are in conversations outside the classroom. The teaching they do shows them that their learning matters to others. We may well be fostering more socially engaged, aware, and active citizens in this country. Not a bad outcome for ten minutes of sharing!

Spoken Reflection

▶ **Four-way share**—This clockwise share typically occurs at a table or desk grouping. The group often has a focus (e.g., how each wrote in a way designed to engage their readers or how each used questioning to understand more deeply).

▶ **Think-pair-share**—Students share thinking about a text or writing target in pairs, then join a group of four to refine thinking, then join another group of four, then share insights with the whole class.

▶ **Partner or trio reflections**—For example, two or three students focus on providing feedback to another writer, discuss a shared text, or engage in joint problem-solving around a sticky spot in a book or writing.

▶ **Open forum**—Students sit in a large circle where they can see each other to direct their own sharing time. They use hand signals to indicate that they would like to share and respectful language to engage with one another (e.g., "Thank you, Matthew, I would like to share"; following sharing, "Would anyone else like to share? Marisol, would you like to share?"). The teacher is only a process observer, providing feedback about what seems to be working and what obstacles the group is facing.

▶ **Using technology**—Students share their thinking about texts and/or their writing and receive feedback from peers using technology. Showing successive drafts of writing is particularly successful and for many children having a peer make comments on a Google document is more productive than having a face-to-face conference with a peer.

▶ **Notice and share**—For example, students observe a group demonstrating how to be helpful in a peer conference followed by sharing observations to the demonstrating group—what worked, what was not as helpful.

▶ **Joint sharing**—Students share with the whole class. Pairs and trios of students share what they have been working on as readers or writers and invite other students to join them in their work.

Figure 8.2 Spoken Reflection

POSTLUDE

This I Know for Sure

In *The Literacy Studio*, I have argued that we can rethink the classic reader's and writer's workshop to encourage students to engage in much more meaningful reading and writing. We need to see reading and writing as flip sides of the same coin. If, during a Crafting Session, for example, we can focus simultaneously on how a reader might use a new strategy or tool and in the next breath show how it is useful to writers, we have begun to transform our teaching toward a more integrated, sensical, and effective model. If, during Composing, students choose whether they will pursue work as a reader or writer first in books and topics they have chosen, their engagement in the work will deepen, and their learning will become more memorable. If, during a Reflecting Session, our students connect their learning to issues and ideas beyond the four walls of a classroom, they will have taken the first step toward using their tools and strategies to understand and build compassion for others in the world. These things I know for sure because I've been fortunate enough to witness each.

In my experience, children adapt quite quickly, to be honest more quickly than the adults, to a new workshop model because an integrated approach simply makes so much sense to them. If I mention that I need to remember to ask questions as I read to make the meaning clearer and longer lasting, a child will, after a couple weeks of practice in Literacy Studio, finish my sentence to say, "And in my writing, I have to get my readers to ask their own questions." I've observed this phenomenon so many times. Elementary-aged children simply have less to unlearn. They don't often see reading and writing as two different subjects—it's we adults who have compartmentalized them. In fact, I notice that our youngest students are often the most adept at thinking about reading and writing at the same time. Perhaps it is because they have spent fewer years learning to bifurcate them.

It is also clear, having worked in dozens of classrooms where teachers employ a Literacy Studio, that children are far more engaged when they have the choice to read or write in a particular time block. I hope I've made it clear that students will ultimately write as much as they read during Composing time, but that the opportunity to choose when to read and when to write matters in an outsized way. Getting to decide where they'll initially try a new strategy or tool—in reading or in writing—helps students build confidence, which in turn bolsters their early attempts in the form of language that is not their first choice. Ultimately, I hope that we will see students working seamlessly as readers and writers, going back and forth, working to apply their own intentions, and simply loving to read and write.

It isn't just about what makes sense and what kids prefer, though. I have tried to show that, at least since the important Tierney and Pearson article, "Toward a Composing Model of Reading," in 1983, we have understood that we want children to approach text, whether as writers or readers, with an active composing stance in mind. Tierney and Pearson suggest that the theory, which grew out of Don Graves' and others' work and is often referred to as "writing process," applies perfectly to reading. We want students to be alive in composing the meaning that is unfolding in their minds as readers just as we want them to compose on the page or when their fingers touch the keyboard.

Researcher Steve Graham (2017) reminds us that readers observe text through a writer's lens, noticing more of the author's moves which in turn calls on the reader to read even more closely and with metacognitive awareness. He describes a cognitive process that becomes habitual, seamless, and mutually beneficial to readers and writers. Why wouldn't we want our students to experience this advantage? Because we adults have long divided the two is not a defensible reason.

Though this book is ultimately about what makes sense to young readers and writers, it is also about what is more efficient, effective, and expedient to us as teachers. With a Literacy Studio model, we can streamline the amount of time during which students receive often duplicative, or worse, unrelated, instruction, giving them more time to read and write independently and us more time to confer and convene small groups, thus differentiating more effectively. In a Literacy Studio, we minimize the number of transitions and maximize the most engaging part of the workshop: the time to read about what excites and fascinates them and to write about what matters most. We no longer have to feel exasperated because we ran out of time for writing again or because we don't have time for students to share their thinking about books. We can actively realize what drew us to teaching and learning in the first place—the chance to immerse children in the joy and challenge of using language to make meaning.

I think back on the day I first outlined this book while sitting in the Rose Reading Room of the New York Public Library. I remember my first few keystrokes and the audacity any author has to have to believe that those first words will find their way into readers' hands. Pulling one's thoughts and experiences together for a book isn't easy. (I suppose that sentence defines "stating the obvious.") There is just so much more I could have said, so many more tips and tricks, so many stories of children living in a Literacy Studio. But I will say, unapologetically, that I am not a "tips and tricks" writer, not a "tips and tricks" educator.

But there is something I know for sure.

Since the publication of my first book in 1997, *Mosaic of Thought*, coauthored with Susan Zimmermann, I have found that teachers, instructional coaches, principals, and central office leaders in curriculum and instruction have been the ones who really write my books. It is practitioners like you and those all over the world who bring these ideas and theories to life. Every classroom teacher who puts their own spin on the ball, every educator who reworks my words on the pages of a book into something relevant to their students—these are the true authors of this and every other book I've written. As I write, I know that the practices I propose in this book will be stretched and adjusted, revised, and developed far more than I could possibly describe—this is what I want. I will hear about interpretations that I won't particularly like, but I am a fierce proponent for each teacher's right to make those changes. No one, no one, who isn't living in your classroom should tell you what and how to teach. We can advise, but never direct. You are highly trained, responsible, creative, and most importantly, an astute observer of your students. You know them, you adjust teaching practices to meet their needs, you care deeply about their welfare.

I am, however, profoundly grateful and humbled by the fact that you are willing to try, that you are up for having a go with the ideas I share in this book. I view myself as a theorist, in many ways. I draw on wells of research, ideas, experiences, and a great deal of demonstration teaching in classrooms all over the world, but I am no longer responsible for a group of students every day. I have been immensely fortunate to have had the opportunity to study literacy through digesting research and trying ideas on for size in classrooms, to observe and teach in hundreds of classrooms alongside extraordinarily gifted educators, and to learn from the leading thinkers in our field. I consider myself lucky to have the opportunity to work with children nearly every week of the school year. I am fascinated by language use and devour every opportunity to study children at work in classrooms, to confer with them about their language use, and to amend my theories and practices based on what I learn from them.

And now you must decide how to adapt the practices I've proposed in this book to your students' needs. You will discover the adjustments that will make the Literacy Studio sing in your context. I know this for sure. It has happened with every book I've written.

I think about you with something like awe, particularly following years like 2020 and 2021. You were able to pivot to remote learning over a weekend, you found ways to engage students who never turned their cameras on, you were able to wrap students in the warm embrace of your concern for them as human beings at a time when we all found ourselves off-balance and frightened. You put your own priorities on the back burner to serve your students, your workdays became twenty-four hours long, you forged relationships with students in the most difficult of circumstances, and you still found a way to nurture your own families. It was hard. It was imperfect. You are exhausted. And it's teaching, so of course it will continue to be hard, and you will continue to find a way to invite students into in-depth learning that will stay with them for a lifetime.

As we reflect on the year that was, it is my sincere hope that we will be willing to embrace ever more significant change in our classrooms and schools. I, like you, am committed to ensuring that we are fiercely attuned to students' needs, that we strive for equity in our work with students from every race and family background, that we speak out against injustices our students face, and that we take seriously the responsibility of opening every educational opportunity to all students. All means all, as I wrote in *To Understand* (2008). All means all.

If you can do that, you can make this book your own. Adapt, revise, tinker, argue with it, find your own way into what I propose, make it better. For all these reasons, I entrust this book to your study, your interpretation, your knowledge of children, your wisdom. You will make this book your own. This I know for sure.

Classroom Name/Date _____

Learning Target _____

Thinking Strategy _____

Evidence of Learning _____

Crafting

Composing • Independent Reading and/or Writing

Check-in

Reflecting

Student Record: Daily Reading and Writing Record

Name _____ Week of _____

Today I chose to:	**Read** Title of my text	**Write** I'm working in my notebook/working on something to polish or publish (circle one)	**Confer** with my teacher/set goals or intentions (what I'm working on as a reader or writer)
Monday			
Tuesday			
Wednesday			
Thursday			
Friday			
On my own/reading and writing outside school			

Student Record: Goals and Conference Notes

Name _____

Current class goal	My intention	Notes from a conference	Questions/things to discuss in my next conference
Date	Date		
Date	Date		
Date	Date		
Date	Date		
Date	Date		

Student Weekly Thinking Record: Narrative Reading and Writing

Name _____ Week of _____

What I'm reading: _____

What I'm writing: _____

Narrative reading

Class goal: _____

My reading intentions (what I'm working on as a reader): _____

_____

You may wish to record questions, ideas that are confusing, connections to life experiences, world knowledge or other texts, your ideas about key themes, sensory or emotional images, ways in which you change your thinking as you read further, inferences, opinions, new ideas that emerge as you reread particular sections: _____

_____

_____

_____

My thinking about what I'm reading: _____

_____

_____

You may wish to ask for help on something you're trying as a reader: _____

_____

_____

_____

Narrative Writing

Class Goal: _____

My writing intentions (what I'm working on as a writer): _____

_____

_____

My audience is _____

_____

My purpose is _____

_____

My plans for this piece of writing:

_____ Polish

_____ Publish

_____ Continue to develop ideas in my notebook

You may wish to ask for help on something you're trying as a writer:

_____

_____

_____

_____

_____

_____

Student Weekly Thinking Record: Informational Text Reading and Writing

Name _____ Week of _____

What I'm reading: _____

What I'm writing: _____

Informational Text Reading

Class goal: _____

My reading intentions: _____

Record your questions, ideas about key content or themes, confusing or unfamiliar words and/
or content, your synthesis after reading, insights about the structure of the text itself. What
are the key content ideas you learned from your nonfiction reading this week?

_____

_____

_____

_____

_____

_____

_____

_____

_____

_____

Informational Text Writing

My writing intentions (what I'm working on as a writer): _____

_____

_____

My audience is _____

_____

My purpose is _____

_____

My plans for this piece of writing:

_____ Polish

_____ Publish

_____ Continue to develop ideas in my notebook

You may wish to ask for help on something you're trying as a writer:

_____

_____

_____

_____

_____

_____

Student Weekly Thinking Record

What did you learn about yourself as a reader this week?

_____

_____

_____

_____

What did you learn about yourself as a writer this week?

_____

_____

_____

_____

How can your teacher support you?

_____

_____

_____

_____

What are your goals/intentions for next week?

_____

_____

_____

_____

Teacher Record Keeping: Teacher Conference Record Reading and Writing

Name _____ Date _____

Text or written piece: _____

Class goal (teacher)/student progress toward it Present performance	Goal(s) for next conference	Observations/next steps Date for next conference/group work?
Student intention (new or following up) Present performance	Student intention for next conference	Date for next conference

References

Allen, P. A. 2009. *Conferring: The Keystone of Reader's Workshop*. Portsmouth, NH: Stenhouse.

Allington, R. L. 2011. *What Really Matters for Struggling Readers: Designing Research-Based Programs*, 3rd ed. New York: Pearson.

Anderson, C. 2018. *A Teacher's Guide to Writing Conferences*. Portsmouth, NH: Heinemann.

———. 2000. *How's It Going: A Practical Guide to Conferring with Student Writers*. Portsmouth, NH: Heinemann.

Bennett, S. 2007. *That Workshop Book: New Systems and Structures for Classrooms That Read, Write, and Think*. Portsmouth, NH: Heinemann.

Bishop, R. S. 1990. "Mirrors, Windows, and Sliding Glass Doors." *Perspectives: Choosing and Using Books for the Classroom* 6 (3). https://scenicregional.org/wp-content/uploads/2017/08/Mirrors-Windows-and-Sliding-Glass-Doors.pdf.

Bomer, K. 2010. *Hidden Gems: Naming and Teaching from the Brilliance in Every Student's Writing*. Portsmouth, NH: Heinemann.

Bomer, K., and C. Arens. 2020. *A Teacher's Guide to Writing Workshop Essentials: Time, Choice, Response*. Portsmouth, NH: Heinemann.

España, C., and L. Yadira Herrera. 2020. *En Comunidad: Lessons for Centering the Voices and Experiences of Bilingual Latinx Students*. Portsmouth, NH: Heinemann.

Fitzgerald, J., and T. Shanahan. 2000. "Reading and Writing Relations and Their Development." *Educational Psychologist* 35(1): 39–50. DOI: 10.1207/S15326985EP3501_5.

Fletcher, R. n.d. "The Benefits of Keeping a Writer's Notebook." *The Writing Masters* (blog series) Heinemann. https://blog.heinemann.com/writingmasters-fletcher1. Accessed April 19, 2022.

Fletcher, R., and J. Portalupi. 2006. *Craft Lessons: Teaching Writing K–8*. Portsmouth, NH: Stenhouse.

Fountas, I., and G. S. Pinnell. 2012/2013. "Guided Reading: The Romance and the Reality." *The Reading Teacher* 66 (4): 268–84.

Glover, M. 2019. *Craft and Process Studies: Units That Provide Writers with a Choice of Genre*. Portsmouth, NH: Heinemann.

Golden, M., ed. 2011. *The Word: Black Writers Talk About the Transformative Power of Reading and Writing*. New York: Crown.

Goudvis, A., S. Harvey, and B. Buhrow. 2019. *Inquiry Illuminated; Researcher's Workshop Across the Curriculum*. Portsmouth, NH: Heinemann.

Graham, S. 2017. "What Is the Relatonship Between Reading & Writing? It's Linear." teachthought blog. https://www.teachthought.com/literacy/better -readers.

Graves, D. H. 1983. *Writing: Teachers and Children at Work*. Portsmouth, NH: Heinemann.

Guthrie, J. T., and A. Wigfield. 2000. "Engagement and Motivation in Reading." In *Handbook of Reading Research*, Vol. 3, edited by P. B. Mosenthal, M. L. Kamil, P. D. Pearson, and R. Barr, 403–22. Mahwah, NJ: Lawrence Erlbaum.

Hall, C. 2021. *The Writer's Mindset: Six Stances That Promote Authentic Revision*. Portsmouth, NH: Heinemann.

Hansen, J. 2001. *When Writers Read*, 2nd ed. Portsmouth, NH: Heinemann.

Harvey, S., A. Ward, M. Hoddinott, and S. Carroll. 2021. *Intervention Reinvention: A Volume-Based Approach to Reading Success*. New York: Scholastic.

Hindley, J. 1996. *In the Company of Children*. Portsmouth, NH: Stenhouse.

Ivey, G., and P. H. Johnston. 2013. "Engagement with Young Adult Literature: Outcomes and Processes." *Reading Research Quarterly* 48 (3): 255–75.

Keene, E. O. 2008. *To Understand: New Horizons in Reading Comprehension*. Portsmouth, NH: Heinemann.

———. 2012. *Talk About Understanding: Rethinking Classroom Talk to Enhance Comprehension*. Portsmouth, NH: Heinemann.

———. 2018. *Engaging Children: Igniting a Drive for Deeper Learning*. Portsmouth, NH: Heinemann.

Keene, E. O., and S. Zimmermann. 1997, 2007. *Mosaic of Thought: The Power of Comprehension Strategy Instruction*. Portsmouth, NH: Heinemann.

Knapp, M. S., and associates. 1995. *Teaching for Meaning in High-Poverty Classrooms*. New York: Teachers College Press.

Lightman, A. 2019. *Three Flames*. Berkeley, CA: Counterpoint Press.

McTighe, J., and G. Wiggins. 2013. *Essential Questions: Opening Doors to Student Understanding*. Alexandria, VA: ASCD.

Miller, D. 2018. *What's the Best That Can Happen? New Possibilities for Teachers and Readers*. Portsmouth, NH: Heinemann.

Miller, D., and B. Moss. 2013. *No More Independent Reading Without Support*. Portsmouth, NH: Heinemann.

Morrow, L. M., D. H. Tracey, D. G. Woo, and M. Pressley. 1999. "Characteristics of Exemplary First-Grade Literacy Instruction." *The Reading Teacher* 52 (5): 462–76.

National Governors Association Center for Best Practices, Council of Chief State School Officers. 2010. Common Core State Standards. Washington, DC: National Governors Association Center for Best Practices, Council of Chief State School Officers.

Pressley, M., L. Yokoi, J. Rankin, R. Wharton-McDonald, and J. Mistretta. 1997. "A Survey of the Instructional Practices of Grade 5 Teachers Nominated as Effective in Promoting Literacy." *Scientific Studies of Reading,* 1 (2): 145–60. DOI: 10.1207/s1532799xssr0102_3.

Ray, K., and M. Glover. 2008. *Already Ready: Nurturing Writers in Preschool and Kindergarten.* Portsmouth, NH: Heinemann.

Reis, H. T., K. M. Sheldon, S. L. Gable, J. Roscoe, and R. N. Ryan. 2000. "Daily Well-Being: The Role of Autonomy, Competence, and Relatedness." *Personality and Social Psychology Bulletin* 26 (4): 419–35. DOI: 10.1177/0146167200266002.

Rosenshine, B. 1995. "Advances in Research on Instruction." *The Journal of Educational Research* 88 (5): 262–68.

Shanahan, T. 2006. "Relations Among Oral Language, Reading, and Writing Development." In *Handbook of Writing Research*, edited by C. A. MacArthur, S. Graham, and J. Fitzgerald, 171–83. New York: Guilford Press.

Taylor, B. M., B. J. Frye, and G. M. Maruyama. 1990. "Time Spent Reading and Reading Growth." *American Educational Research Journal* 27 (2): 351–62.

Tierney, R. J., and P. D. Pearson. 1983. "Toward a Composing Model of Reading." *Reading Education Report No. 43.* Champaign, IL: University of Illinois at Urbana-Champaign.

Tierney, R. J., and T. Shanahan. 1991. "Research on the Reading–Writing Relationship: Interactions, Transactions, and Outcomes." In *Handbook of Reading Research,* Vol. 2, edited by R. Barr, M. L. Kamil, P. B. Mosenthal, and P. D. Pearson, 246–80. Mahwah, NJ: Lawrence Erlbaum.

Wharton-McDonald, R., M. Pressley, and J. M. Hampston, 1998. "Literacy Instruction in Nine First-Grade Classrooms: Teacher Characteristics and Student Achievement." *The Elementary School Journal* 99 (2): 101–28. DOI: 10.1086/461918.

Children's Books

Boynton, S. 1982. *Moo, Baa, La La La!* New York: Little Simon.

Dyckman, A., and Z. OHora. 2015. *Wolfie the Bunny.* New York: Little Brown Books for Young Readers.

Hall, D., and B. Moser. 1994. *I Am the Dog I Am the Cat*. New York: Dial Books.

Honda, T. 1995. *Wild Horse Winter*. San Francisco: Chronicle Books.

Jenkins, M., and V. White. 2010. *Ape*. Somerville, MA: Candlewick.

Morales, Y. 2018. *Dreamers*. New York: Neal Porter Books.

Muth, J. 2002. *The Three Questions*. New York: Scholastic Press.

Nelson, K. 2013. *Nelson Mandela*. New York: Katherine Tegen Books.

Park, F., G. Park, and C. Zhong-Yuan Zhang. 2000. *The Royal Bee*. New York: Boyds Mills.

Steptoe, J. 2016. *Radiant Child: The Story of Young Artist Jean-Michel Basquiat*. New York: Little Brown Books for Young Readers.

Thomson, B. 2010. *Chalk*. New York: Two Lions.

Williams, K. L., and K. Mohammed. 2007. *Four Feet, Two Sandals*. Grand Rapids, MI: Eerdmans Books for Young Readers.

Woodson, J. 2014. *Brown Girl Dreaming*. New York: Nancy Paulsen Books.

Wyeth, S. D., and C. K. Soentpiet. 2002. *Something Beautiful*. Northfield, MN: Dragonfly Press.